Reviews for Wil

--Filled with lots of magical ways bit of storytelling keeping alive your eyes open for the faceless n more of this book, in fact, I neve Susanna for a wonderfully warm, cosy magical read. Now I'm off to read some more of her books

--Folklore, storytellers, devotion to the Old Ways, herbal healing and the beautiful wildflower garden are some of the aspects that add enchantment, mystery and romance to this book. There is also an element of the Fae that excited my imagination. Beautifully written by this skilled Yorkshire author, I highly recommend this book. And of course, there is a huge dog, a magnificent stallion and a handsome fellow.

-- I thoroughly enjoyed Flora's story. Like Flora, I've always had an affinity with animals and nature. I enjoy using natural remedies and that comes from my Irish mother. I enjoyed Flora's friends and family and of course, Finn, Fury, Freya and Rowan. Cal sounds like a bit of alright too!

-- An Enchanting modern faerie story- it carries the reader down a gently babbling brook to the inevitable happy ending! Read it in the Sunshine with the soundtrack of birdsong - a definite potion for a blessed day.

-- A lovely, light-hearted mystery with witches & magic set in a quaint village surrounded by nature, very well written and explains the craft and witches in a modern & understanding way. I LOVED THIS READ!

-- What a great read! Join Flora at Gallipot cottage in the village of Farstone as she starts a new life in her Aunt Sybil's home as its new owner. Meeting a whole cast of characters from the local community, fae magic & learning about her true identity and how her wildflower ways are indeed her true calling. With a dark handsome stranger on a black steed and a big friendly hound, it's a truly special book

Susanna Scott lives in a seaside town on the Yorkshire Coast and enjoys Nature, gardening, trees, reading - and being with her family.

Also by Susanna Scott -
The Gypsy Caravan
The Winterfell Stone
Weavers Green
Acorn Cottage Christmas
Druid's Oak Farm
Wildflower Witch

*

The Chalk Tower - a Reverend Grace Danton cosy crime mystery.

*

And for children -
Robin Hood and the Wolfshead Tree

Susanna Scott @yorkshirecoastwriter on Facebook.

The

MIDWINTER

SPIRIT

Susanna Scott

Copyright © Susanna Scott 2024
All rights reserved

ISBN: 9798343670660

For my mum and dad
Marjorie and Arthur Scott.
With love.

In the bleak Midwinter
Frosty wind made moan;
Earth stood hard as iron,
Water like a stone;
Snow had fallen, snow on snow.
Snow on snow,
In the bleak Midwinter
Long ago.

Christina Rossetti

Chapter 1

December 16th

Edward Fynch-Stratton stood on the steps of Midwinter Hall staring into the distance across the fields. He looked like a tall, tanned, Greek God with blond hair, blue eyes and aristocratic good looks. Except his expression now was more Severus Snape on a bad day and when Bridie followed his line of sight she saw why. Stomping back across the field towards her own house was his neighbour, Zinnia Pelham and they had obviously had words. Again.

What worried Bridie more was that he had now turned his attention to the first of the large greenhouses, where she was currently sharing a pot of tea with Henry the ancient gardener, instead of being hard at work cataloguing the extensive library in the Hall. She grabbed her mug and went to hide behind the Swiss Cheese plant in Henry's 'office', whispering a quick. 'I'm not here' to him as she did so. She heard her boss come in all bustle and hubris.

'Have you seen Miss Emms?'

She'd worked here for a month and it was still Miss Emms. She called him Ned. Not usually to his face though as she needed the job. You could hear the hesitation in Henry's voice.

'Miss Emms? Er, Bridie?'

He was a lousy liar, mostly because he believed in telling the truth. Ned put him out of his misery.

'Miss Emms.' he called out in a resigned voice.

Bridie sidled out from behind a large leaf and took a sip of her tea, smiling hopefully. The Greek God whose skin was shown to be weathered with working outdoors and whose hair now looked like a faded blond without a Grecian curl in sight, sighed heavily.

'I've just been looking in the library for you.' he said accusingly, his brow lowered.

'I'm on my lunch break.' she tried.

He looked at his watch.

'At 10:50 in the morning'.

'Elevenses?'

He frowned more deeply.

'Early elevenses? I have to get up and walk around for 10 minutes every 2 hours and so I walked out here to–'

'Miss Emms.'

He put his hand up to stop her.

'Bridie, please' she smiled pleasantly. He ignored her.

'Have you come across any deeds, land searches or surveys in your work?'

She thought for a moment or two.

'There are lots of histories of Midwinter Hall that go back right to the building of the place. I'm not sure if any of them mention what you need. Do you want me to check?'

'If it's not too much bother Miss Emms but please, do finish your tea first. If you wait another five minutes you might actually be able to call it elevenses.'

Ooh, she thought, if your tongue gets any sharper, you'll be able to cut up your food as you eat it. She took the hint and swallowed the rest of the tea quickly as he turned and stalked off back to the hall. She seemed permanently on the edge of being dismissed.

'Troubles brewing. Mrs Pelham's not been the same since her husband Emlyn died. She used to love all animals.' Henry shook his head gravely.

'Is it about his top field again? The one he wants for the donkeys?'

'Ah well, that's just it you see. That's the problem. They're both claiming it. And you'd better get back and prove it's Sir Edward's.'

Bridie grinned. Old Henry was the only one who ever gave him his title and then only when he remembered. It even seemed to embarrass Ned himself who insisted he call him Ned, which he did more often than not now. Ned wore his title lightly, like a jacket that he could put on if needed officially but which mostly lay discarded. Henry had worked for Bertie Fynch-Stratton, or Sir Albert, Ned's father, and was firmly in the old school, who showed respect for their bosses. Unlike her, it would seem.

'Yes Sah!' she saluted and ran off back to the oak-panelled library and the old, priceless tomes to be found there.

It had been a waste of a day. After a fruitless search where she learnt more about Midwinter Hall than she ever wanted to, all she ended up with were tables full of books and a now almost defunct filing system.

Bridie Emms, ex-bookshop owner with a degree in History and a Masters in Historical Research, was beginning to hate the sight of old books. Her bookshop had specialised in old, out-of-print books and there was an online business attached to it, searching for hard-to-find books. It was quite a niche market and she sold classics and contemporary books to offset this but it didn't stop the business running at a loss.

Eventually, she had to sell all her stock off to pay her debts and although selling them was what she was supposed to be doing in the first place, she was still sad to see them go. Some of them were old friends and had been with her for years, which was exactly why she'd got herself into this mess in the first place.

She still rented the small flat above the shop, which was now a beautician's salon specialising in 'Plump lips', 'Beautifully Perfect Nails' and 'Soft, Smooth Waxed Legs' and other vacuous things. What added insult to injury was that, however, vacuous, the shop was now doing a roaring trade with customers who would find it hard to read a book - presuming they *could* read - because of the black caterpillar lashes stuck on their upper eyelids.

She was sounding very bitter and she had to stop this train of thought. People had a perfect right to make their money through the beauty trade as she had through the book trade. She thought she might be bitter too as the deeply-tanned and sparkly Belaire sisters were not only doing better than she had – but were very likeable too. Damn them. She had a good natter with them over coffee every week. Her bookshop was no more – it was unrecognisable as the same place.

Bridie looked around at the overloaded tables and dismissing her former love of books, decided that she wouldn't care if she never saw another old book in her life. There were references to the building of the Hall and the land around it but nothing specific enough for what he wanted. She wasn't looking forward to relaying this information to Ned Fynch-Stratton if he was still in the same mood. Perhaps he had calmed down by now.

On cue, Ned appeared at the glass-paned door and his frown entered the room a split second before the rest of him. Bridie cringed.

'Well, found anything?'

'Nothing concrete so far.'

'Have you looked everywhere?'

'Not yet?' she replied lightly 'but I was worried the tables would collapse if I added any more books.'

She gestured theatrically at the groaning tables with their slim, Georgian legs. He paused, obviously wondering what else he could complain about. He found something.

'Do you know what you're looking for? Some of the sections are in Latin. I don't expect you to understand but you could put a marker in so that I can read it. Are there many more of these to go through do you think? Bloody woman!'

This last was said as an aside and though he probably felt the same about her, this will have been directed at his neighbour, Zinnia Pelham, whose obstinacy he blamed for the problems.

'Yes, there are quite a few more I believe but they will have to wait until Tuesday now, when I'm in again. I'm not really sure you'll find what you're looking for here though. Have you tried your solicitors?'

'Oh, what a good idea. I wish I thought of that. Just think of the time it would have saved me.'

Bridie set her teeth at this sarcasm and mentally kicked herself.

'You've already been on to them then?' she said.

'First thing I did. Nothing. Yet my father always said it was ours.'

Bridie moved to pick up one of the lighter books, to lock it away behind steel-netted glass doors before she left.

'You can leave them all out. I'll check them over.'

Bridie swung her coat on, grabbed her bag and made for the door. She turned as she reached it and addressed his back as he leant over the books.

'Spero te inverire omnia quae quaeris, praesertim verba Latina.'

His body went still and then he half turned towards, her a smile playing on his lips.

'Scis ergo Latinum?'

'Yes, I do know Latin' she replied, 'as part of my history degree but mostly through my Masters in Historical Research. You read my C.V. – that's Curriculum Vitae – 'course of life' translated from the Latin– I presume?'

He raised his eyebrows.

'I glanced at it. I was desperate and you seemed to know what you were doing, despite being a bit ditzy. That's what the week's trial was for and you passed with flying colours.'

Bridie chose to ignore the compliment.

'A bit ditzy?' she said incredulously, even though she knew the accusation had been levelled at her before, possibly with justification.

He suddenly grinned disarmingly.

'You sometimes come across as a bit – eccentric maybe? A lot of intelligent people I know are quite mad.' If he was going for damage limitation, she wasn't sure it was working. 'As to your earlier Latin statement, I hope I find what I'm looking for too but not especially the Latin words now that I know you can translate them as well as I can.'

She smiled and turned to go.

'Bridie?'

Her eyes widened and she drew a sharp intake of breath. It was the first time he had called her that. When she turned back to him, her face showed no surprise.

'Yes, Ned?'

His eyebrows shot up again. He obviously wasn't used to being made fun of, but then he started laughing – and she joined in. Then he nodded in the direction of the front door.

'Be careful driving home, they've forecast snow.'

Chapter 2

December 20th

The promised snow had arrived later that night and by morning, everywhere was covered. Luckily, Bridie had the whole weekend plus the Monday, when she didn't have to go to work. She only worked four days at Midwinter Hall.

So now as she looked out of her flat window, the snow was only on one side of the pavement, the one with no sun. Some remained at the sides of the road where it had been snowploughed. She had also sent a text to Stella, one of the girls who worked in the huge main greenhouse, to find out what it was like out there and she had told her the roads were mostly clear. Midwinter Nurseries was a good 10 miles away in the middle of the countryside and she had been worried it was worse there but everyone else had managed to get into work.

'When 'Bridie's Books' had closed, she had needed a job straight away and didn't care what it was. Money was going to be very tight. Unfortunately, this was the beginning of November in a town that was dead in winter. She was just about to throw herself on the mercy of the government benefit system when help came in the guise of one of her old customers, Clement Ball, who loved old musty books as much as she did.

Edward Fynch-Stratton had a library of leather and cloth-bound books and he hadn't a clue what, or where, most of them were as they weren't in any sort of order. Clement who had known Ned's father, told him he would help him catalogue them but soon realised the enormity of the task. The library ran across the whole of one side of the building - and it was a large building.

He had suggested Bridie for the temporary job and Ned was impressed that she had dealt with old and precious books before. That's probably why he hadn't bothered looking at the qualifications on her CV. He had still insisted on an interview though. She smiled to herself as she remembered him standing and holding out his hand offering her the job, saying 'at least I know you'll be careful with my books'. Then she had sprung up to shake his hand and knocked the remains of her coffee all over the papers on his desk. She apologised profusely whilst laughing which didn't go down well. He looked like he regretted the job offer, so she bid a hasty retreat and with a jaunty 'See you on Tuesday', she left before he could take it back.

She'd been pretty good since though - apart from... She spluttered, remembering Mr Popple and croissant crumbs flew all over her table. Mr Popple. The name itself, although she didn't know why – little things amused her - made her laugh, especially when Mrs H, the cook and housekeeper, told her his first name was Hugo. Hugo Popple. She grinned again now, although she did think she'd lost her job that time.

The girl who cleaned through and helped in the kitchen had been off work that day and Ned was annoyed as he needed to impress Hugo in order to clinch the new local authority contract. Mrs H suggested that Bridie could serve tea and cakes to them. Ned had looked horrified, she had no idea why, but grudgingly he accepted the help, with the warning not to spill tea over his important client or do anything else to upset him. Bridie looked innocently hurt and Ned had raised his eyes to heaven.

She had served tea without incident. sending a 'See!' look in her boss's direction. It was when she went to collect the tea tray that it all went wrong. As she bent over to put the cups on the tray, she could feel a hand creeping up her leg under her skirt. She froze as he started to caress her backside and then she glanced at Ned, who she could have slapped for being so unaware, as he gave her a puzzled look.

She couldn't help it. Her mother had said the devil got into her at times. Without moving, she said loudly,

'Oh excuse me, Mr Popple. It seems your hand has somehow got stuck to my arse. Do you need help to remove it?'

Hugo Popple flung himself against the chair back like he'd been physically struck by a sledgehammer. Ned shot up as Bridie exited, tray half-full, as she was sure she'd get told off or probably dismissed. As she started to walk down the hallway, however, she was encouraged and very pleased to hear Ned tell the old lech,

'I don't think I want to do business with your type after all. I would like you to leave now. I would tell you to apologise to the lady but I doubt she'll want to set eyes on you again - and neither do I.'

Bridie now laughed and shook her head at the memory. It had all ended well as Mr Popple had been fired, Midwinter Nurseries had landed the contract and she'd kept her job.

As Bridie turned off the main road and drove towards Midwinter Hall, she could see that the snow had more of a hold here. She had become a mine of useless information since trawling through the books. They were mostly about Midwinter Hall and the history and geography associated with the district around it. The Hall had been built in the 1700s for the Fynch family who were gentlemen farmers and passed, through the last Fynch, to the daughter. She married into the aristocratic Strattons and the house had remained in the Fynch-Stratton family today, as ably demonstrated by Ned Fynch-Stratton himself.

Although still minor aristocracy, he now had to earn his own living and very successful he'd been too. The upkeep of the Hall, which was just a large Georgian house, was where most of the money went. It was his passion and Bridie had to admit he was doing a good job of maintaining it. The parts she'd seen anyway. Ned's other passion was horticulture. Bulbs and seedlings were grown in one of the great greenhouses and bedding plants in another, all to be sold on, in their various stages, to retail garden centres and local councils for their parks and gardens. Outside, in large fertile fields, seasonal flowers were grown to supply florists, garages and supermarkets.

The wide grassy valley where Midwinter Nurseries stood, created a microclimate which gave perfect conditions for flower growing. Ned worked outside in the fields in all weathers, which accounted for his tanned, weather-beaten look, with his crinkly, light blue eyes shining out. He looked every bit the farmer his Fynch ancestors had been, apart from they would have had farm workers to do it for them. Ned actually liked to get stuck into the work with his fellow workers. Bridie admired him for that.

The nearer she got to Midwinter, the worse the snow was and the approach on the minor road was down to a single track. Luckily it was mainly delivery vans and nursery workers who used it. Granted, it was popular with people out for a relaxing drive in the glorious countryside, but she didn't think there would be many of those today. She took it slowly and breathed a sigh of relief as she reached the open iron gates without meeting another car.

Midwinter Hall looked so pretty in the snow. Four Georgian windows below with a central porticoed entrance which had columns on either side and a tiled roof above. Above the top five windows, on the roof, was a central triangular pediment with a small window. At either side of the driveway, near to the house, stood two conical-shaped trees about twelve feet tall. White Pine, according to Henry, although they had an attractive blue tinge to them. Snow still decorated every branch.

As she slithered her way down the first part of the almost white driveway, she found Marcus Wendell, the driver/handyman/jack of all trades, in the middle of clearing the drive. He backed the mini digger to the side so she could pass.

'Hi Marcus, have you done this just for me? It's very kind of you.' she shouted through the window and he grinned back at her. Possibly in his late fifties and withdrawn by nature, he might not have had much to say but she could always coax a smile out of him.

'Have all the workers made it in today?'

' Most on 'em.'

He nodded at her as she waved and she continued down to her parking spot. She was glad everyone had made it today as it was a busy time just now for the nurseries. Where most of their rivals eased off at this point, Midwinter was kept busy providing the material for wreaths, to florists over a wide area and for Christmas decorations in important council and other large buildings.

There was a special holly grove on the estate. Not originally grown for this purpose, but part of Midwinter's outer grounds from generations ago. It nestled under the shelter of taller oak trees, where conditions were perfect for its growth and it now provided perfect holly for the whole of the Yorkshire Wolds.

In fact, Ned was known amongst his clients as the Holly King. The go-to person for winter decorations. Ivy was provided too as it grew freely up the oak trees, Oaks seemingly providing ideal growing conditions for all Christmas greenery and this included mistletoe, with the clusters sprouting magically from the upper branches. When the pine branches from the fir trees on the valley ridge behind the hall were included, they provided all that was needed for their busy Christmas period.

As she made her way around to the front of the house after parking up, she laughed as she saw Little and Large come out to greet her. Tamsin, the Border Collie raced happily across the snow, tongue hanging out of one side of the permanently smiling mouth. She planted wet paws over Bridie's coat.

'Have you missed me girl?' she asked as she hugged her.

Looking up. she laughed even more as she saw Tink picking her way carefully through the snow with a disgusted look on her face. Tinkerbell, Tink for short, was a dainty Yorkshire Terrier, inherited from Ned's godmother when she died. Ned had shortened her name as he refused to shout out Tinkerbell in public, although people still smiled when he shouted Tink anyway. She soon became one of the family, the most aristocratic of them all. That didn't stop her from jumping into Bridie's arms as she reached her. She gave the tiny dog a cuddle, receiving a lick on her nose in exchange - and all three went into the warmth of the Hall.

Chapter 3

Still December 20th.

'Carry on looking for evidence of ownership of the Top field today. We need it quickly.'

Bridie turned around to see Ned searching in a huge hall cupboard with his back to her. Without a hint of diplomacy, the two dogs hurriedly transferred their allegiance to their master. Bridie couldn't think for the life of her why they loved him so much as most of the time he was a miserable grump. She took off her coat and hung it on the antique wooden coat stand then went down to the library. As she turned to shut the door, he was behind her.

'If you find anything, however small, bring it to me.' He hesitated, eyeing the heavy tomes on the table, 'or let me know and I'll come here.'

'Okay' she said and she tried very hard not to carry on talking - but she'd been thinking about it over the weekend...

'Ned?' she said to his retreating back. She knew she was pushing it as he stopped abruptly and she could almost feel the expression on his face. By the time he turned around, he had rearranged his features into an expression of resigned acceptance.

'Yes?' he said.

'Why has it got to be before Christmas? What's the hurry?'

The very audible sigh was one of frustration, as though he told her many times before but he hadn't. Not once. Even Mrs H. hadn't mentioned it and she knew everything.

'Because the sanctuary has let me know that the donkeys are being delivered on the 23rd and I need the field by then.'

'Is there shelter in the top field for them?'

He looked uncomfortable.

'Not yet. I'll have to bring them back through the old oak wood across from the holly grove and down the track to the stables here.'

'Why can't you just turn them out in the field behind the stables with Bessie?'

Another exaggerated sigh.

'Bessie is nervous around other horses. She won't accept them. I tried to get her to accept other horses in the past but she won't have anything to do with them. It stresses her and I won't have anything upsetting her.'

'Donkeys aren't horses, exactly' said Bridie.

'Sam and Etta Bradley, from the farm over the valley tried to keep their donkeys in the field when they went away for three weeks. Bessie went crazy. She wouldn't entertain their company. They had to find somewhere else.'

'What about the parkland in front of the Hall?'

'It's not secure. It's open to the road up at the top to provide ease of access for all our delivery vans. It would cost a fortune to provide secure fencing and we'd still have the problem of the open gateway. And, before you ask, yes, we could take them up the driveway and along the road but it's a detour of a couple of miles that way, twice a day - and we'd still need permission to go through Zinnia's land. I'm not having the donkeys going through all that – or Bessie unsettled in her later years.'

He stared at her for a moment, waiting for her to question this, but she knew how much Bessie meant to him. Mrs H. had told her that Bessie had been his workhorse and he used to ride her around his estate. Even now, when she was older and he had a quad bike, he used her on days like today when she was sure-footed and less liable to slip than his quad bike. She was also still as strong as an ox with huge carthorse-like hooves. You wouldn't think she was such a sensitive little soul with other animals. Maybe she'd been bullied by other horses before he rescued her. She was okay with the dogs though. Well, she tolerated them at least.

Ned had made it to the door and had almost closed it.

'Ned?'

'Oh, for god's sake, what now?'

'Have you ever thought that perhaps you can't find evidence that the top field is yours because it isn't?'

He put his hand to his forehead and pushed his floppy, unruly quiff back.

'Of course I've thought that. Zinnia and I are both convinced that the field is ours. The only saving grace is that she can't find any evidence of ownership either. Although she says she's seen it years ago. It's not even the ownership of the field itself that bothers me. It's why she is so determined that two homeless, badly-treated donkeys shouldn't use it. The Zinnia I knew before -and of whom I was very fond believe it or not - would have jumped at the chance to rehome them.'

He shook his head and was just about to head off again when he turned.

'Anything else?' he asked with heavy irony.

'Nope,' she replied and looking like he didn't believe her he backed out slowly.

Bridie felt a bit disloyal. She'd only been here a month and didn't owe her boss that much loyalty - but he had given her a chance with the job - and she did quite like him. He was growing on her, was probably the best way of putting it.

The reason she felt disloyal was that on her first day here when Ned had been called out on business just before she arrived, she'd been sent by Henry to have a walk around the estate to familiarise herself with it. Never mind that she would be chained to the library shelves most of the time.

*

It had been a bright November day and she found herself heading to her left, up over the parkland in front of the Hall. She found a grassy track, one that led from somewhere behind Midwinter Hall. She carried on walking until she could see woods spread out at either side of the track. Continuing upwards on the track which now had trees at either side, she saw the wood on her right was made up of oak trees with thickets of holly underneath them. The holly trees were a few feet taller than her and the red berries were out on most of them, providing colour against the green spiky leaves.

The track that ran down the middle separated the holly trees on her right from another wood to her left. That wood was a completely different entity. The trees were still oaks but much more ancient, taller, wider and more majestic. That wood was very quiet. Eerily so.

Bridie stood on the edge. Looking down the untrodden grass path through this wood and somehow felt it would be sacrilege to enter it. She had laughed at herself but still stayed where she was, listening to the complete silence which almost hurt her ears. She wasn't superstitious. She didn't have a fanciful bone in her body, yet she found herself reluctant to disturb that stillness.

She remembered that after a few minutes the atmosphere changed and she looked further down that path to see a woman walking towards her. She had long grey wavy hair clipped back with combs at either side and had on a long brown skirt which brushed the floor as she walked. She smiled knowingly as she came up to Bridie.

'Didn't you want to enter the wood?' she asked.

She had on long dangly earrings and a heavy perfume hung around her. She reminded Bridie of her mum, who was a hippie throwback too. Bridie smiled back at her.

'I didn't want to disturb it. Don't ask me why' she laughed raising her eyes to heaven.

'It's all right because I feel the same. I do feel like I've trespassed today but I have good reason. In any case, the wood knows I have only good intentions towards it and that I respect its sanctity.'

Okaay... thought Bridie. Possibly she is *very* hippie/New Age - or even as mad as a March Hare.

'So, you decided to wait outside the wood?' The woman asked her and with that, she realised that she could probably join her at the Mad Hatter's tea party.

'Yes.' Bridie looked sheepish. The woman laughed.

'My cats agree with you. They're both sat at the other end of the wood, waiting till I come back out. They won't enter it.'

She held her hand out.

'Zinnia Pelham.'

'Bridie Emms, pleased to meet you'

Chapter 4

Zinnia's Story

The two women walked down the path together towards the hall. After Zinnia remarked that she might not want to mention meeting her as she was going to tear a strip off Ned Fynch-Stratton - and after Bridie explained that it was her first day and she had no idea what was going on... they fell into an easy conversation.

Zinnia explained the ownership - or non-ownership - situation and added,

'It isn't the donkeys. I love donkeys and horses and dogs and cats. It's not the field itself.'

Zinnia frowned and fell silent - and unusually for Bridie, she didn't interrupt this silence with questions. It paid off. Zinnia turned towards her with a questioning look.

'You knew there was something different about the Silent Wood, didn't you? You respected it?'

Bridie thought that this was a very apt name for the wood.

'I suppose I did in a way. I'm not too much into feelings of that nature, so it must have been strong to make even me feel its power.'

Zinnia put her hand on the younger woman's arm and smiled triumphantly.

'There, you see!'

Bridie didn't but the woman looked so euphoric, she didn't want to disappoint her. Then Zinnia started to tell a tale as though she had a full audience instead of someone who just wondered what she'd got herself into.

'It's the wood itself that I'm trying to protect. This wood is all that is left of an ancient woodland, the rest chopped down for building houses, for fuel and to make way for agriculture and pasture for animals. I'm not saying it was wrong exactly because it was what was needed in those early times I suppose. Yet this ancient Oak wood has been here since long before Midwinter Hall was built and long before man took ownership of the woods - which should belong to no one – or everyone and certainly not to one person.

'The path running through the middle of it is an ancient trackway and probably used by the Druids for ceremonial purposes. It originally ran almost in a straight line from the valley behind the Hall, over the hill with the pine trees, round the back of the hall, up through this track we're walking on and then through the old oak wood. It carries on past my place, which was the estate manager's house for the Hall and then peters out somewhere between the B-road at the top of our land and the main road.

'Legend has it - and I believe it - that this oak wood was a Druid's Grove within the woods, where they worshipped. It escaped being chopped down as men would have refused the task as it was considered sacred and it would have brought bad luck on whoever chopped them down. I love trees. I love woods. Yet I can feel the difference between other woods and this one. This one is special. I know that from personal experience.'

Zinnia stopped and looked embarrassed then quickly carried on.

'So you can perhaps understand why I'm against this. To get to the field - whether it's his or mine is largely irrelevant - someone would have to tramp through the wood at least twice a day, to and from the Hall stables. Yes, I know the workers collect holly, ivy and mistletoe from the oaks in the other wood for the wreaths but that's for a few weeks in December. They leave the other wood alone for, I imagine, the same reason we do, even though there is ivy growing up the trees and mistletoe hanging from the boughs just the same. No holly though – that's only in the 'new' wood.

'I once came through the Silent Wood and on down the track to see Ned, when we were on friendlier terms.' She suddenly looked sad. 'A couple of the workers were collecting the stuff at the edge of the new wood and no one was saying a word. It was as if they knew, like those woodcutters from all those years ago that this place was different. If the wood was used regularly it would suffer. Lose its tranquillity. Lose its... Magic. It's selfish of me I know and quite loopy I suppose from another's point of view but…'

She turned to Bridie in desperation.

'Oh, do you understand what I mean?'

Bridie looked at this woman. Her crazy long wavy hair arrayed around her shoulders like a lion's mane. She saw the pleading look in her wild, pale eyes and she smiled.

'Unfortunately' The other woman's shoulders sagged. 'I think I do.'

Zinnia looked surprised, then hugged her in a bear hug, while Bridie wondered privately if *she* was going loopy too. Still, as always, she had spoken from the heart and without thinking first, which she had found was just another way of telling the truth.

Chapter 5

December 21st
Midwinter Solstice

Bridie arrived first thing and initially was glad not to be searching through any more books that weighed a ton - but when she found she was to be working in an almost windowless attic, she was less enthusiastic.

Thinking about her first conversation with Zinnia had made her wonder if they were looking for proof of ownership of the top field (called the bottom field by Zinnia), in the wrong place.

She didn't want to take sides at all. She liked both the antagonists, but neither did she want to go fruitlessly searching in the library, upsetting all her carefully catalogued books. She had emailed and suggested to Ned that perhaps the proof would be found not in documents from when Midwinter Hall was built but from when the old estate manager's house, Midwinter Lodge, was sold into private ownership - well before Zinnia and her husband bought it. Surely if there was any allotting of land it would have been then.

Ned had jumped on this suggestion, calling himself all the idiots under the sun and emailed back, promising to sort it out in the morning.

He was as good as his word and led the way up two flights of stairs to the attic. This space had one window, which was covered with thick snow and had turned to ice.

Firstly, Bridie asked if she could open the window to get rid of the solid snow. At least then she could have a view while she was being bored stiff. Ned refused saying that the window hadn't been opened in years and would in all probability fall out and kill someone passing by. (Passing by? she thought.) Besides, what was wrong with the electric lights?

Thwarted by this she at least got him back by asking why on earth he had stored documents in an attic. He answered by saying that when his father died he needed to get rid of all the documents over 100 years old, to make more room in his office. He had found archival-quality storage boxes and shoved everything up here.

As she couldn't think of anything else to annoy him. She got on with the business of searching through many, many boxes of old documents which was possibly worse than the library books.

After a couple of hours, she went downstairs in search of coffee. The vast kitchen, at 11:00 a.m., always smelled tantalisingly of freshly roasted coffee which the boss insisted on.

'Ah, there you are my love. Didn't think it'd be too long till you poked your nose in here. Do me a favour would you m'dear? Take this out to Henry.'

Mrs H, she wouldn't let you call her Yvette as she wore the fond nickname like a badge, was an old retainer like Henry. Having worked for Ned's father as Henry had, she was now past retirement age. The 'master' kept her on and viewed her almost like a mother substitute, as his own mother had died when he was young. She still held on to the small flat at the back of the first floor with the stairs leading directly down to the kitchen.

Bridie was fond of Mrs H, with her steel grey curls in a hairspray-helmet and her chubby-cheeked, ruddy face always ready to break into a smile, she seemed more like a mother figure to Bridie too. Her own mother was too busy saving the world along with her father in Morocco or wherever they were at the time.

They had gone over to save something or other years ago and left Bridie at boarding school, only seeing her when she went over to them in the school holidays. Boarding schools should she say? She had managed to get expelled from the first one. Some of the teachers did not appreciate her sense of humour. You wouldn't have thought that Halloween would have brought out the sensitive, nervous side of the Maths and Biology. mistresses or that they would have jumped into the lake to get away from the 'Spectre' - or that the biology mistress couldn't swim...

Anyway, Mrs H was the mother she would have chosen if she could. She took the big mug of tea, never coffee for him, and the scone then went thankfully over to Henry, one of her favourite people, in the first greenhouse.

'Oh lovely. Just what the doctor ordered lass' he smiled. taking the steaming mug from her. Even though there was a kettle, a tea-making necessity there, he looked forward to his twice daily cuppa from Mrs H., a testament to how much the Midwinter family meant to each other. Marcus Wendell, the Jack of all Trades was included, although he never had much to say for himself. His wife had left him six years ago before he worked here and he had some sort of a breakdown. Ned had taken him on and Marcus had repaid him with unswerving loyalty ever since. In fact, the more she thought about it, the better Ned appeared to her. Saving handymen, saving5 donkeys, saving dogs...

'Is Rose okay Henry?' she asked.

Henry and his wife Rose had lived in a little cottage on the edge of the estate for as long as anyone could remember. Rose was a lovely, smiley little lady. Apparently, her little home was spotless and Henry's tea was on the table at 5:15 p.m. on the dot as soon as he got in. It was easy for Bridie to dismiss this old-fashioned vision of the perfect housewife, but since she had worked here she realised she had rarely seen a couple as happy and contented as Henry and Rose.

'Aye, she's fine lass, thanks for asking. How's your job going?'

'Don't ask. He's got me imprisoned in the attic now like the madwoman in Jane Eyre, or Bob Cratchit, working all hours with hardly any light and no coal in the fireplace.'

Henry laughed.

'No fireplace either in the attic as I remember and the heat rises. I reckon you'll be warm enough' he smiled knowingly.

'I'm bored enough, that's for sure. I wish they'd just come to an agreement. What is wrong with them?'

He looked sad.

'I don't know Bridie. I wish I did. They used to be good friends. Let's hope the Christmas spirit finds them soon.'

'Let's hope', she answered crossing her fingers in front of her. She went back to the hall following the smell of the coffee but something else called her attention.

Ned was standing in the doorway of the drawing room having a conversation with someone inside. She had heard a car making its way up the driveway as she was in the greenhouse. He looked like he couldn't wait to be rid of whoever it was. Peering past him, she recognised Neville Blanchard, the oily supercilious, patronising solicitor who represented Zinnia Pelham. Bridie had taken an immediate dislike to him the previous week when he had treated her like a skivvy who had little or no intelligence. He thought he could show his superiority by using long words that he hoped would confuse you. He never used one of these words when three would do, usually ending with 'Indubitably' to prove his point when questioned over the truth of his wordy statements.

Bridie had listened to him with the library door open and didn't know whether to fall asleep with boredom or give him a book on how to condense your words so you don't sound like a complete prat. She could hear him now. She could even hear an 'Indubitably' float over Ned's head towards her. He set her teeth on edge and she could feel her hands forming into fists.

'I don't actually care what you or your partners think,' Ned was saying, 'the fact remains that ownership hasn't been established on either side.'

'Yet, as the fair and no doubt, intelligent person you appear to be, you are forced to acknowledge that my valued and respected client Mrs Zinnia Pelham remembers the phrase 'including the bottom field' in her dealings with the original acquirement of the property known as Midwinter Lodge.'

'Remembering is not the same as having written proof.'

'Indubitably, Sir Edward, yet…' he gave a pathetic little slimy bow which made Bridie want to go over and strangle him. 'I see you have not yet furnished us with verification of your *own* right of possession of the said area which is under debate, generally known by you as top field.'

You could hear that it hurt him to say anything as plain as top field. She imagined he would prefer to say the Pinnacle of Green Open Space. She smiled to herself.

'I will be doing so, believe me' said Ned.

'I would anticipate the interaction but my respected principal, Mr Ballantine and I are of the opinion that the said debated land is the rightful property of Mrs Zinnia Pelham, indubitably.'

As Bridie didn't have any sellotape handy to cover her mouth she set forth to make her presence known.

'I declare that opinion to be factually inaccurate. Wouldn't you tend to concur with my considered statement, Sir Edward?' she said, trying for the same supercilious tone that Blanchard attained. Ned turned to her and the corners of his mouth twitched.

'I would say that your own statement is more factual than the previous one attributed to Mr Ballantyne by our learned and esteemed visitor.'

Neville Blanchard now stood in the doorway with a puzzled look on his face. Bridie and Ned faced each other.

'Indubitably' they said together.

Bridie doubled over with laughter, happy that he was on the same wavelength.

As the affronted Mr Blanchard stamped out, Ned called after him,

'And tell Mrs Pelham that I deal with no one but her from now on.'

'Or from this moment in time and henceforward' shouted Bridie, while Ned collapsed against the wall, his laughter echoing around the hallway.

Mrs H, emerging silently from the kitchen, observed them both.

'Silly beggars' she said, before leaving their coffee mugs on the hall table.

Chapter 6

December 21st – Winter Solstice
Afternoon

The attic was feeling stuffy now and since Ned had disappeared over an hour ago, Bridie decided she was ready for a visit to the kitchen. Checking the time she realised the visit was overdue. It was just gone 2:00 p.m. and her tummy was rumbling.

She had found no evidence of ownership. Other fields were mentioned. The top field and interestingly, the old oak wood too, seemed to be a sort of no man's land. Perhaps this was true and the field didn't belong to anyone She was keeping this thought to herself as they may still find evidence, but while things remained at an impasse she didn't want to jump the gun on something that may not be correct.

She could smell the polish as she headed down the stairs. Kitty had given the place a thorough clean and would have headed home by now. Today was the last day of foraging for Christmas vegetation, as most of it would already be woven into wreaths and winter floral displays.

Two of the men were dropping a vanload off in Bridie's town today and then Marcus was making a special delivery tomorrow to the local stately home a few miles further down the valley, in time for their annual Christmas Eve ball. Everyone but Marcus who lived in a flat above the old stables and Mrs H, would be finishing work today and wouldn't be back until Wednesday the 4th of January. There was nothing for them to do and they received full pay for the time off plus a Christmas bonus.

Thinking of this she nipped across to the greenhouses first to say goodbye to whoever was left there. She gave Henry a hug, which made him blush and he told her he'd probably come up and check on the seedlings and bulbs he'd already set going. You couldn't keep him away from the place.

Reaching the kitchen, wonderful aromas were coming from the large Aga.

'Mmm!' Bridie sniffed the air like the Bisto kid.

'Mince pies – to freeze' said Mrs H.

'What, all of them?'

Bridie couldn't keep the disappointment out of her voice.

'No, don't worry' laughed Mrs H. 'I've kept one batch out. Yours is on a tray over there along with a ham sandwich. I thought you'd have been in before now.'

'Oh, Mrs H.' Bridie put a hand to her forehead as though she were in a Victorian melodrama. 'He has me working up there in the attic. No food, nothing to drink. Wearing threadbare clothes'

She wailed and put her head on Mrs H.'s shoulder.

'I've only just managed to escape his clutches. Don't tell on me, kind lady. Please say you won't' Mrs H patted her on the shoulder and went towards the oven.

'There's one thing for sure. You're never in danger of winning an Oscar.'

'How about an award for overacting?'

'You'd win that, hands down' she said, her shoulders shaking as she couldn't hold the laughter in anymore. 'Go and get your lunch before you starve to death, you poor waif.'

'Thanks, Mrs H, you're a good 'un.'

She had eaten the food and was just finishing the mug of tea when Ned rushed in. Have you seen Fred?' he said addressing Mrs H until he saw Bridie. 'Never mind you'll have to do.'

'It's so nice to feel wanted' she said.

'Can you go to the holly grove for me? I've got to see Terry and Phil off with the last load. The hospital has just phoned. Fred's wife slipped on their path and she's broken her arm. It's already been sorted but she needs him to drive her home. It's over in Bewsholme. She's okay, they say. Take the dogs with you.'

He rushed out again. The snow might have cleared from the roads, but it was bound to be worse underfoot on the grass and the paths. She called to the dogs but only Tamsin appeared. Bridie opened the front door and at this, Tink hurtled through not wanting to be left out, even if she had to suffer for it.

'Good job I brought my walking boots' she said resignedly to Mrs H. before going to the car and fishing them out, along with her thick coat in the back seat. They set out over the snow-covered grass, tramping across it, following the footsteps of the last few workers in the wood. She occasionally lost sight of Tink where the snow was thickest until Tamsin reached her head down and pulled her out by the scruff, setting her down in a more accessible part. After this happened a few times. Bridie gave up and picked the tiny dog up to carry her.

Reaching the main track towards the woods she set Tinkerbell down and putting her hands in her pockets, she trudged up towards the wood.

As the entrance to each wood came in sight, she watched Tamsin who had run on ahead. She stopped at the entrance to the Silent Wood as Zinnia called it and sat down. Maybe she's like Zinnia's cats, thought Bridie.

The next minute, Tink flew past her as fast as her little legs would carry her and was about to career into the wood when Tamsin calmly headed her off. She herded her backwards until the little Yorkie sat down then turned around and sat next to her.

'Brilliant work, Tam' said Bridie as she passed, stroking the dog's head. 'You too' she laughed as Tink looked up at her, wanting her praise too.

She looked to her right into the holly grove to where she could see the figure of a man adding to a heap of greenery on the ground. When she was nearly upon him, the man suddenly realised she was there and nearly jumped out of his skin.

'Jesus! You scared the life out of me. It's Bridie isn't it?'

She hadn't spoken to him before but she recognised him from back at the nurseries.

'I am. Are you the only one left working here?' This must be Fred then.

'The other two left an hour ago. They're loading the van.'

She was looking at the canvas sheet.

'Are you going to carry that on your back?'

'I could. It's big but it's light. No, I'm going to pull these threaded ropes up look,' he demonstrated '– and then drag it behind me. It's easier in these conditions.'

'Oh, good idea.'

He looked at her. 'I've just about finished' he said uncertainly.

'Great' she said looking up at the tree. There seemed to be a lot of ivy there still. There must have been loads before.

'Was… was there anything you wanted? Is everything okay?'

'Fine' she answered distractedly, then suddenly came to full awareness. 'Oh, actually it's not. Your wife is in hospital. I've been sent to tell you.'

'Oh my God' said Fred in a panic. 'Is it bad? What's happened?'

Bridie realised she wasn't making a good job of this.

'Don't worry. Well not too much anyway. She slipped on some ice and she's broken her arm. It's okay. She's had it set but she's stuck at Bewsholme Hospital and needs you to give her a lift back.'

He blew out a long breath.

'That's not too bad. I suppose. Better than I was thinking anyway.'

'Sorry...' Bridie apologised.

'No, thanks for coming out here for me. I'll get off and drag this back then. To tell you the truth. I'll be glad to get out of here. It's the same every year. It's spooky in that wood opposite.' He looked over there warily. 'Don't you think?'

'Don't know about spooky but there's definitely something about it' she replied.

'Yon two agree with me' he said nodding at the statue-like figures of the dogs. 'They won't go in.'

He tied up the makeshift canvas sledge and turned to her.

'Are you walking with me?'

'No, I'll stay behind for a few minutes. I haven't been in the woods properly before.'

He looked at her as though she was mad.

'Don't stay long. It'll be dark soon. Shortest day today. It's the Winter Solstice' and he disappeared silently towards the track.

Chapter 7

Winter Solstice - Silent Wood

Bridie hadn't wanted to mention this to Fred but she had seen a glimmer halfway down the wood. She wasn't sure if it was Zinnia with a torch or a trick of the light, but she didn't want to spook Fred any more than he already was.

Luckily she didn't scare so easily. She had been the only one of her friends who stayed in a supposedly haunted house for the full night. The others went back in daylight the next morning to see if her brains had been sucked out and she had been changed into a zombie. She sensed their disappointment when she came out of the door laughing. It wasn't that she didn't believe in the supernatural, in fact, she hoped it did exist. It was just that she was a sceptic and needed things to be proved to her. For such a - Ned's word came unbidden - ditzy person, she had a very logical mind. You see, even now, her logical mind whilst dismissing supernatural happenings without proof, had to admit that there must be more to life. More things to see, feel and prove than the facts they already knew.

She had reached the place where she'd seen the light. There was a large oak tree on her right, taller and wider than the others. The light seemed to be coming from that.

'Hello,' she whispered.

The tree shivered, its branches moved as though caught in a breeze though there was no breeze here. She watched, taken aback, as a young woman stepped out, seemingly from behind the tree and proceeded to cross the grass path in the middle to get to the other side of it. She completely ignored Bridie. The girl was halfway across when Bridie said again.

'Hello, who are you? Can I help?'

The girl turned to her now, a confused expression on her face.

'Are you all right?' Bridie had already decided she must have escaped from somewhere secure. She was wearing a long luminous white dress and no coat. Incredibly, she was also barefoot. A wreath of ivy and mistletoe was wound around her head. She glanced back at the tree and saw that the light had gone. The glow from the girl's dress was what she must have seen.

'You can see me?'

The girl's voice made her jump, its tone and accent were so unusual. She had to strain to hear her, she was so quiet, her voice seeming to come from a long way away. Despite her worries about the girl, this statement made her smile.

'I'd have a hard time missing you in that dress, wouldn't I? You look like a glowworm in human form. You're not a ghost, are you?' she added, only half in jest.

Now it was the girl's turn to smile. It was a lovely smile, even through the faintly green make-up she had on her face. Then she laughed. A sparkly little laugh, like rainwater over pebbles.

'I'm not what *you* would call a ghost.'

'What I really meant was – is that what you're supposed to be? Are you going to a fancy dress party?'

'A celebration? Others dressed in their finery, oak and holly?'

'A Christmas party then?'

'Midwinter?' the girl replied distractedly and began moving away slowly in the direction she had been going before, towards the thickest part of the woods.

'Can I walk with you? ' said Bridie, going after her.' You must be freezing. Here, take my coat.'

The girl smiled a serene smile which suddenly seemed to make her appear older.

'I am not cold, I can promise you this. It is only a little way.'

She lifted an arm to point to the southwest, where the last vestiges of a watery sun were spreading in pale orange against a dark grey sky.

'Take care then' Bridie frowned, not at all convinced she should leave this obviously innocent and vulnerable young woman - but short of dragging her back to the Hall, like Fred's holly and ivy sledge, what could she do?

The girl smiled her calm, benevolent smile and, leaning forward, put her hand on Bridie's arm. There was a sudden warmth.

'See, I don't feel the cold.'

Bridie was now worried that the girl had a temperature and was burning up. Her next words put her mind at rest.

'Please, do not worry about me, although it is very kind of you. I can assure you, there is no need.'

Bridie looked into her soft, golden eyes and knew she was telling the truth.

'What is your name?' the girl asked

'Bridie, what's yours?'

The girl said something that sounded like Derry.

'Pleased to meet you, Derry.'

She received a last smile and then Derry disappeared into the woods, accompanied by the glow that surrounded her. Bridie felt she had been picked up and dropped down in the middle of a Fairy Tale. Shaking her head to dispel that thought, she watched the glow until it disappeared. When she turned back to the path, she realised it was dark.

Turning her phone's torch on, she navigated down the path to pick the two dogs up. Literally, in Tink's case. Unusually, for a very obedient dog, Tamsin had to be called three times as she just sat there, staring into the wood. Perhaps she had seen the strange light coming off Derry's dress too.

On the way back down the main track, she reflected on the meeting. She thought of radiation with the white luminous dress with the green tinge. She thought of phosphorescence emitted from trees as a natural reaction. She thought of the oddly warm touch on her arm. She hadn't actually felt the touch, just the heat. The girl had seemed relatively normal to talk to – if 'otherworldly', despite her appearance, then that made her think of aliens. How normal was it though, to be wandering around a wood at sunset in a flimsy robe when there was snow on the ground?

Her lack of sensitivity to so-called phenomena was being put to the test and she was starting to wonder if there was more to this encounter than was obvious.

She turned into the parkland and ahead of her, she could see another light, hovering in mid-air. What was going on tonight? Halloween hadn't changed to December 21st had it? Suddenly, she knew what this light was as Tink leapt out of her arms and both dogs ran towards the light.

'There you are' came Ned's relieved voice. 'Thank goodness! I was beginning to think you had been abducted by aliens.'

His laugh was forced, borne out of relief probably. Although it would have been the dogs he was more concerned about. Aliens? Well, maybe that's what Derry was after all. She mentally slapped her wrist. She had reached Ned now.

'It's nice to know that you cared' she grinned and, although she couldn't make out his expression properly in the shadow, she could tell by the slight dip of his head that he was blushing.

*

'You want me in tomorrow?' she wailed. Bridie had just refused the offer of a hot chocolate because she wanted to get home. No rain had fallen but what snow was streaked across the roads would be icy now. It seemed worse in the dark somehow.

'I- yes- I thought you knew?'

Ned looked like he was trying to remember if he had mentioned it before.

'No, everyone else finished work today so I naturally assumed...'

'That's because there's nothing left for them to do in the nurseries. Mrs H is still cooking, Marcus is doing the last delivery to the Crichton's place tomorrow and you...'

He had the grace to look embarrassed. He'd obviously just assumed she knew.

'Well, the donkeys arrive the day after tomorrow. We need to finish the search of the attic. Last ditch attempt. As soon as we find evidence, then you can go home early.'

'Good of you' she said, hands on hips.

Was she pushing it? No, he really did look very apologetic and she knew how much it meant to him.

'Okay, see you in the morning then. I expect to be met with a hot chocolate though. '

He gave a tentative smile.

'Drive carefully' he said.

She nodded, then nothing ventured nothing gained, she asked

'Do you know a girl called Derry from around here?'

He looked at her quickly and frowned.

'Very pretty, slim, strange. She was in the woods and said she was going to a party.'

'Our woods? A party? '

He still looked shifty. As though he were hiding a secret horde of treasure in the woods and this girl was his accomplice.

'Yes, some sort of celebration maybe? '

Was that a sigh of relief she heard from Ned?

'Ah, where was she headed?'

Bridie turned around to get her bearings and then pointed in the same direction the girl had gone.

'Was she in her late teens? Brown hair?'

'I think so '

Now, looking back, she wasn't actually sure of the colour of her hair. The impression was that she was young. She couldn't get a clear picture of the girl in her mind.

'It might have been a fancy dress party?'

'That sounds like the Rushtons. They own the farm over that way. You won't have noticed it as you drive in from the opposite direction. Huge family - uncles, aunties, brothers, sisters-in-law. copious children. Always having family get-togethers. Always inviting me too, or did until they realised I'm basically unsociable and it's not my sort of thing. Lovely family though. This girl will be one of the granddaughters, she visits a lot. Seen her a couple of times but can't remember her name.'

Well, that explained it all, thought Bridie. Aliens? Ghosts? Earth to Bridie, you can come back now! She laughed inwardly at her flights of fancy. Waving to Ned, she faced the journey home with little enthusiasm. At least no more snow was forecast. A white Christmas was not on the cards.

Chapter 8

December 22ⁿᵈ

The car's windscreen still needed de-icing but all along the street the sun was shining and hopefully melting the snow that was still left this morning.

It was definitely not going to be a white Christmas if this weather continued. People were opening up their shops with more enthusiasm than they'd had for days. The cafe, further along, risked putting a couple of tables outside for customer's to sit in the sun with their dogs. The greengrocers manhandled a couple of boxes of fruit and veg onto a small trestle table in the hope that they wouldn't freeze solid today.

The same High Street shops had still been open when she got home last night. The lights on in the windows on a cold dark night had cheered her. It had forced her to think about

Christmas though. Eileen's cafe was lit by coloured fairy lights and she had seen the vague figures of people sitting at the steamed-up windows enjoying the warmth before they faced the walk home.

Deepak Saraf's chemist's shop had been brightly lit, with a moving reindeer and a jolly Santa in the window obscuring the queue of people waiting for their last prescriptions before Christmas.

Enzio and Maria's greengrocers had a warm yellow glow in the window supplied by two Christmas elves, each holding a lantern. In between them, the usual banner - 'Support Your Local Shops' - was now partly covered by gold and red tinsel. In pride of place on the door was a wreath they had created from Midwinter Nurseries greenery. Holly with red berries, ivy woven in and out, small fir twigs peeping from the back and mistletoe hanging down the middle. There was a bunch of mistletoe hanging in the shop too, which Enzo had a lot of fun with. Maria just tutted fondly as he kissed the cheeks of many middle-aged matrons and made them blush.

The library at the top of the street had its large window, running the length of the building, full of local children's brightly coloured Christmas paintings.

It had all brought it home for Bridie that Christmas was a few days away. It was a depressing thought. Not that she was trying to emulate Scrooge. She liked the idea of it. It was just a non-starter for her. Her parents had never celebrated it and hadn't even bothered to come home during the festive celebrations. She had fond memories of Christmas at her grandparents' house though, where she enjoyed all the festive fun viewed with a kind of snobbish distaste by her parents.

When the grandparents died, there had been a few drunken Christmases at university, which might have captured the Christmas spirit, if only she could remember them. The rest of the time. she either spent Christmas on her own or with her best friend. And then her best friend and her husband. And then the same couple with the new baby.

This year she had been invited again, but there was a 3-year-old and a 6-month-old baby too. Bridie felt that they would have enough to cope with, especially with both mothers-in-law getting into the usual one-upmanship of how *their* Christmases were the best.

Bridie thought she might just spend it by herself again. It was only one day after all. Still, it was a depressing thought. She would just get the day over with and hunker down. She would get a few bottles of alcohol and some festive ready meals in and prepare to watch the full gamut of Christmas films that were on offer. She was quite a sad case really, she laughed to herself but it would soon be January - and she would have to start thinking about how to earn money when she had finished the cataloguing at Midwinter Hall.

She arrived at the Hall and drove normally without a slither in sight, down the drive, now cleared in the middle thanks to Marcus. She hoped she would get a Christmas bonus from Ned. He was a generous employer yet she needed every penny she could get. There wasn't much work in these parts and she had to find a local job if she wanted to stay around here - and she did. She felt at home in this part of Yorkshire. She wondered if there might be a job going in the greenhouses. One of the girls was pregnant and thought she might leave soon.

She was just going to park near the stables when she realised she could park in one of the open garages further on. One of the 'lads', in reality he was probably in his late '50s, had taken the larger delivery van home with him after they had delivered their last load yesterday. She slid the small car into the garage with plenty of room on either side. Snow wasn't forecast and the sun was shining but better safe than sorry.

Ned and the dogs met her in the hallway.

'Where's my hot chocolate?' she asked.

'I thought coffee would be better this morning. I've made us a flask each and a picnic box full of sandwiches so we can get on with no disturbances.

'If we don't find evidence. Are you going to keep me chained here over Christmas until it's found?'

He laughed uneasily.

'I might ask you to come in tomorrow as well.'

'Oh, you *are* joking?'

She didn't know why she was objecting, she had nothing better to do.

'Well, let's see how we get on today, shall we? Come on then.'

He led the way up to the attic, not even giving Bridie time to take her coat off.

'Slave driver.'

'I heard that.'

'You were meant to.'

Nice backside though, she thought, following him up the stairs.

*

All day he kept her working there until there were only ten boxes left to go through. Imprisoned in the castle turret…okay, stuck in the attic, still with no view through the window. Bridie had lost track of time until her slave driver stopped cracking his whip at last. Yawning, he stretched his arms above his head and then glanced at his watch. He looked surprised and then said,

'Coffee and a late lunch.'

She picked up her phone to check the time. It was almost 2:30 p.m. She tried to check her messages but there was no network. It had been all right yesterday.

'Have you got reception on your mobile?'

'I haven't brought it. I didn't want any distractions. I told Mrs H. not to disturb me today.'

'You might have urgent messages on your phone' she reasoned.

'Nothing is as urgent as this, especially as we still haven't found the evidence we need.'

He placed one of the flasks in front of her and opened the sandwich box.

On the plus side, we haven't found evidence the field *isn't* yours either. What the hell are these?' she asked in astonishment.

'Ham sandwiches' he answered looking hurt, then conceded,

'Mrs H had gone to take some stuff to Rose at the cottage first thing, so I had to make them myself. She bakes her own bread and I'm not too good with the bread knife.'

He looked sheepish but then gamely tucked into one of the doorsteps. Bridie looked at hers and privately wondered if she would put her jaw out attempting a bite. The bread was lovely and soft though and it was proper baked ham with just the right amount of mustard, so she couldn't complain. She pulled a face though when she tasted the coffee. He looked over apologetically.

'Yes, I like my coffee strong.'

'Well you've achieved that but at least it will keep me awake for the last document boxes.'

The coffee warmed her up too. She had been on the point of putting her coat back on as it was getting colder. She would manage without it for these last papers. She would feel warmer for the journey home then.

In the event, those last few boxes took well over an hour. Driving home in the dark again.

What fun! At least she would have nearly two weeks off to recover from the search frenzy of the past few days. Ned slowly picked up the last large manilla folder from the last large grey box. He opened it, read it, and then sat down with his head in his hands.

'What do I do now? I've run out of places to look.'

'Maybe have another word with Zinnia and try to work something out.'

'I can't talk to her. She's obsessed. I don't know what's wrong with the woman.'

He looks so frustrated and hopeless.

'Come on' said Bridie. 'Let's get out of this attic before we go crazy. We need to stretch our legs and I need to get home before it gets too dark.'

He smiled at her as he stood up.

'Thanks for all your help Bridie, I really do appreciate it, even if we didn't get a result. There's an extra bonus in an envelope in my study downstairs. I'll go and get it while you gather your things' and he picked up the empty lunch things to carry them down.

That's good, thought Bridie. He'd already paid the normal Christmas bonus into her bank account as he had with all the others. This must just be for the extra work she'd put in. She supposed it was worth it as every penny counted at the moment.

'What the–' she heard Ned exclaim faintly from downstairs on the landing.

Grabbing her bag, she went down the attic stairs, closing the door at the bottom. As she turned she could see Ned leaning over the banister with a horrified expression on his face. She went to stand next to him and turned to look out of the top hall window to see what was wrong. She soon saw.

There was an early darkness outside, but that didn't stop the moonlight from revealing the sight of a total blanket of snow. No driveway or indeed much else was to be seen. The snow that the weather forecasters said wasn't going to happen, adding apologetically with smiles on their faces, 'No White Christmas this year, I'm afraid folks.'

Oh yes?, thought Bridie with a sharp intake of breath. How wrong could you get?

Ned raced down to open the front door where, despite the open porch, a foot of snow collapsed inwards and fell over his feet. As Bridie joined him to stare out at a scene more suited to Antarctica, the snow began to fall more heavily, thick and fast, until their view was obscured by the snowstorm.

Chapter 9

December 22nd – The Snowstorm

Ned pushed past Bridie in his hurry to get to the kitchen. He flung the door open and both Mrs H and Marcus looked up from their cuppas.

'Why didn't you tell me?' he accused them.

The dogs who had been dozing in front of the Aga had run across to greet him- but stopped dead at his tone and went silently back to their places.

'About what?' Mrs H. was genuinely puzzled.

'About what?' he retorted, 'About the complete white-out outside!'

Mrs H would only stand so much. After all, she'd known him since he was a babe in arms. Her jowls trembled as she stood up.

'Don't you take that tone with me, lad! I didn't tell you about it because, for one thing, I thought you might have seen it for yourself and for another, you told me under no circumstances to disturb you. Now, you can apologise as quick as you like' she lectured and Ned quickly lost his indignation and looked shame-faced.

'I did, didn't I? I apologise unreservedly. It wasn't for my sake that I was angry. Although you weren't to know, we can't see out of that tiny window in the attic, you see.'

Mrs H looked puzzled.

'We?' she asked.

Ned stepped into the kitchen revealing the slight figure of Bridie. She had heard the heated exchange.

'I think he was worrying about how I'd get home' she explained.

'But - But…' Mrs H. spluttered and looked over at Marcus who looked as shocked as she was. 'But what are you *doing* here?' she concluded incredulously.

'Ned asked me to come in to try and find 'top field' evidence. Snow wasn't forecast. It was sunny before we went into the attic.'

'Where's your car?' asked Marcus who didn't usually volunteer a question. 'It wasn't there late morning when I got back from the delivery. Only just made it back too. I thought I was going to have to abandon the van and walk back.'

They all stared at him. That was the most he had ever spoken in one go for as long as Bridie had worked here. At least she came to before the staring got to the point of rudeness.

'Seeing as the larger delivery van wasn't there, I parked in the big garage at the end, so I suppose you wouldn't have seen my car.'

'And your coat wasn't on the hook in the hall where it usually is continued Mrs H, nor your boots on the rack where you usually change to your indoor shoes - and you never mentioned you were working today.'

'I didn't know until just before I got into my car last night and then Ned rushed me up to the attic this morning and I didn't have time to take my coat off. Nor my boots.'

She hesitated, aware that she was making Ned out to be the bad guy. Well actually, at the moment, she felt that wasn't a bad description of him. That soon changed as she watched him sit down at the table and put his head in his hands.

'It's all my fault. Everything's all my fault. Bridie having to work today. Her being stuck here. Me arguing with Zinnia. Me shouting at you Mrs H.'

'And of course, you conjuring up the blizzard conditions to cause this snowstorm and what looks like three feet of snow outside. All your fault! I think I noticed a cat o' nine tails in the attic, we can take it in turns to flog you if you'd like?'

Despite the guilt he was feeling, the corners of Ned's mouth lifted up at Bridie's statements and Mrs H laughed.

'Nay, it's just down to a series of misunderstandings after all. There's one thing, for sure. Bridie is going nowhere tonight.'

It was a measure of how bad things were outside, that nobody questioned this.

'Things might look better in the morning eh?' she nodded towards Bridie

'Put her in my sister's old room can you, Mrs H? It's always aired in case she drops in unexpectedly, you know what she's like. There's lots of her clothes in the wardrobe, so there might be... some sort of nightwear.'

Ned's older sister and her family lived in Scotland but she travelled down here regularly. Bridie hadn't seen her yet.

'Come on. I'll show you to your room and then let's get some hot food into us all.'

As Mrs H. was leading Bridie out of the kitchen, Ned was checking his phone.

'Blast!' he said with feeling.

'What?' asked Bridie.

'Nothing. Only one bar. Bad reception in this sort of weather.'

She gave him the death stare and he gave in.

'Okay. I've found a message sent at 11:00 this morning. It said that the weather is too bad to attempt the journey with the donkeys and it will be after Christmas now.'

Bridie squeezed her eyes shut and opened them very slowly to eyeball Ned who was looking up at her like a particularly pathetic puppy.

'It IS all your fault!' she said loudly before storming off after Mrs H.

*

I don't suppose it's fair to blame him, thought Bridie. Yes, if he'd read that message earlier she needn't to have stayed as it wasn't urgent but it would possibly have been too late by then anyway. If the roads were too bad to bring the donkeys, then the snow must have been fairly widespread around Midwinter Hall.

Of course, with all the narrow country roads leading to it, it would have been much worse here. There was no chance of a gritter either as there were plenty of main routes which would be cleared first so that people could get from one town to another. To use these lanes you had to *want* to reach Midwinter Hall - or the stately home - or one of the farms in the area, as they were all a long detour away from the A-roads. In good weather, this detour was very pleasant. Today. However, you'd have to be a very keen Finnish rally driver to attempt it.

'Go easy on him pet. He gets his mind fixed on something and all else is forgotten. He's got a good heart and he was just worried about you.'

Mrs H who obviously could read minds was pulling clothes from the wardrobe.

'This from the woman who told him not to take that tone of voice with her, 'Lad' 'she added with a grin.

'I'm allowed to' she smiled back holding a nightie up against her.

'I've forgiven him. There is nothing any of us could have done. We can't beat Nature. How tall is his sister?' she said changing the subject as she eyed the nightie.

'Tall' was the reply. 'Nearly six foot, I believe. They're a tall family.'

Bridie estimated Ned was a few inches taller than that. She took the nightie and saw that it trailed on the ground swamping her at 5'5. At least they seem to be the same dress size horizontally, if not vertically. Mrs H. pulled out another one and handed it to her. It might have been a shorty nighty on its owner, coming down to her knees but it was halfway down Bridie's calf.

'This will do' she said, although the virginal white. fastened up to the neck, Victorian nightie wasn't her style - but thinking about her love life or lack of it for the last 5 years, maybe it ought to be.

Mrs H turned the duvet back as though she was used to turning a fresh white sheet back instead and laid the nightie out on the bed. Thanks, Mrs H. Do I *have* to call you Mrs H?'

' I've been called that for almost fifty years now, since not long after I married my Kenneth, God bless him.'

Her husband had died over eight years before and used to do the job Marcus did now.

'I'm too old to change now. Besides, I never thought Yvette suited me. Don't get me wrong, it's a lovely name but it always makes me think of a French starlet in Hollywood'

'Random thought!' laughed Bridie.

'Dinner in an hour after you've freshened up. You can eat in the kitchen with me. It will be nice to have some company for a change.'

'Okay Mrs H - and it will be nice to get away from my ready meals for a change too.'

Mrs H. went out smiling.

Bridie wondered about the eating arrangements. Why did Mrs H eat on her own? Surely in a place with only two people who had known each other for years, they would eat together or even have Marcus join them.

Oh well. She would be more than happy to provide company for the motherly cook. She was the sort of mother that everyone would like. Kind, humorous, stood no nonsense and made lovely cakes, scones, pies and bread. Bridie's mouth started watering. She wondered about getting a shower but then she would have to put these clothes back on. She had a wash, brushed her hair and renewed her lipstick.

Thinking of mothers reminded her of her own who was doing good works in Morocco at the moment. She was definitely a good person but was she a good mother? Bridie didn't want to seem disloyal because her parents loved her in their way - but when she thought of a few Christmases stuck in boarding schools, she had to admit that she wasn't high on her mother's list of priorities. She always wondered if she was a mistake and was slightly resented.

Still, she was old enough now that it didn't matter anymore. She would be thirty next year, almost three weeks after Ned's own thirtieth birthday. He had told her so at the interview as he noticed her date of birth. She had said 'Oh, are you an Aries then?' and he had given her a withering look as if to say 'Star signs? Really?'

As she passed the open wardrobe on the way out, she noticed a fair amount of clothes hanging there and wondered if she should have showered and changed, then she shrugged. She would shower in the morning and climb back into these clothes knowing that she would be going home, if she could just reach the main roads.

Chapter 10

December 23rd

The next morning, Bridie got up early, looked out of the window then went to the wardrobe to pick out something to wear. There was no way she was going anywhere in this. If anything, the snow was even deeper.

She had drifted off to sleep eventually, accompanied by the sound of the wind carrying spinning gusts of snow in a wild, whirling pirouette until it was deposited on the ground. There were no footprints anywhere outside to disturb the pure dazzling white snow showing up against the beautiful but threatening dark blue and pink sky.

She was now completely starkers on her way to get a shower. She hadn't fancied wearing someone else's knickers clean or not, but luckily she found an unopened packet of ten on one of the wardrobe shelves. She would just buy his sister another to replace it. There was a cream Aran jumper and a pair of long jeans that she could roll up. There was also a new bra, but it was a size or two smaller than Bridie wore. It was underwired and lacy too - a world away from Bridie's sensible bras, worn for comfort. She had laid all the clothes, including a dark blue pair of the new knickers, also lacy... on the bed for when she'd showered.

She was just making her way across the carpet to the ensuite when there was a gentle knock at the door. Realising that she hadn't locked it last night, she flew across to the bed in a panic and dragged the duvet off to hold up against her, scattering the neatly laid-out clothes. She had just pulled it up under her chin when the door opened slightly.

Ned's voice said 'Bridie', softly and he poked his head tentatively around the door. He seemed alarmed at the pink-quilted apparition in front of him looking like a giant prawn.

'Oh, er, I'm sorry to disturb you' he said apologetically, 'but I wondered if you'd seen the snow outside yet. It doesn't look like you'll be going home again today. I'm so sorry.'

She didn't want him to start on the apologies again.

'It's all right. Nothing's spoiling.'

'I thought you might be going somewhere today. Shopping or plans involving family and friends?'

'I don't have any family in this country and my friends are mostly married and live away. Shopping - I can always get the chicken breasts out of the freezer if I miss buying Christmas dinner. It's no big deal' she added as she saw his surprised expression.

She must have sounded a sad case. Was she a sad case? He suddenly bobbed down to the floor and came up with the blue lacy knickers hanging on one finger. He smiled in a weirdly flirty fashion.

'You dropped these.'

Was that a double entendre or innuendo? She'd soon wipe the grin off his face.

'Yes, I'm having to borrow them. They're your sister's.'

'Eurgh' he said in distaste, dropping them back on the floor and turned to get the hell out of the room. Then he realised and turned back.

'Oh, the main reason I came upstairs. Mrs H says she'll have a full English breakfast on the table in half an hour. Reckons it will warm us all up.'

'Thank you! I'll be there. I ate so much last night' - the piece of pie on her dinner plate would have lasted her for three meals normally - 'but I have to say I'm starving again.'

'Good. Well, I'll let you get on then.'

'Sorry about the...' And she indicated the duvet she was wearing.

'Not at all. It's been - interesting - talking to the front half of a pink blancmange.'

He was giving her that strange smile again. She frowned and he made a swift exit, still with that annoying smile.

Shower now, thought Bridie, then Mrs H's breakfast. And what did he mean by 'interesting'? Looking over her shoulder, she caught sight of herself in the dressing table mirror immediately behind her – and saw her bottom exposed in all its glory.

*

The two dogs made a huge fuss of her as she entered the kitchen. Happy to find that there was now another inhabitant of the house to make a fuss of them. She was glad of this as Ned was in there waiting for his breakfast and it gave her the excuse to crouch down to them and avoid his eyes.

'That smells good' she said, going over to the Aga and risking a glance at Ned. Luckily he looked almost as embarrassed as she felt.

'Right, get your plates' Mrs H responded and they both grabbed a plate from the warming rack and held it out, like Oliver Twist but with the expectation of getting something much tastier than gruel.

Bridie took hers back to the table where two places had been laid. Hang on, *two* places? She caught Ned as he put his plate on a tray and picked it up.

'You're not leaving us, are you?'

He looked down at his tray and then up at her guiltily.

'I always eat at the table in my office.'

'Not when you have guests, surely?'

She tried for the guilt trip approach.

'Well….' He looked at Mrs H in a mute appeal but she pointedly ignored him.

'Especially when we have to discuss work. The donkey situation. The top field. Documents.'

Reluctantly he took the plate, knife, fork and HP sauce off the tray and sat down at the table.

'I think we've flogged that particular issue to death' he said sadly, 'there's nowhere else we can look here. I'll go through the files in my office once again today on the off chance I've missed something but otherwise…'

'What are you going to do if you can't find anything?'

'Oh, I'll still fight her. She's just being stubborn.'

Bridie and Mrs H looked at each other and the unspoken words 'She's not the only one', hung in the air between them.

'What will I do all day then?' Bridie whined.

'What would you normally do at home?'

Slob around in my jimjams watching corny hallmark Christmas films, open a bottle of wine, eat crumpets with half a tub of butter on them and play sad songs so I can wallow in self-pity, she thought.

'I'd probably read' was what she actually said.

'Well, there are lots of books in my study to choose from. Modern books' he emphasised. 'Help yourself.'

They tucked into the delicious breakfast – bacon, sausages, perfectly cooked eggs with just the right amount of dippiness, homemade hash browns the onions crisped-up with frying, mushrooms, tomatoes, baked beans, and tasty fried bread. The whole thing must have had more calories than a deep-fried Mars bar but was infinitely more satisfying. Bridie sat back.

'I'm stuffed' she said.

Mrs H got up from the table and started clearing it.

' If you want to work your breakfast off. you could help Ned.'

'To do what?'

'He's going to clear a path down to Henry and Rose's Cottage.'

'Don't tell me Henry wants to check the greenhouses in this weather' asked Bridie. He was famous for his dedication to the plants.

'He probably does, knowing him but it's because the oil delivery couldn't get through yesterday, nor the delivery van from Flume's grocers in the town, that they always have before Christmas. Looking out there' Mrs H nodded towards the window. its square panes picturesquely built up with snow in each corner like a Victorian Christmas card. 'it won't happen today either.'

'Oh no, they'll be frozen!' Bridie said in alarm.

'It's not quite that bad' explained Ned. 'We can't provide the oil for the range oven they have but we can take extra fuel for their fire.

There's a hot plate on top of the wood burner that they can use for basic cooking until the order arrives. We're also taking them a cooked chicken and some veg. Plus some of Mrs H's bread and pies. They won't freeze or starve, don't worry.'

Ned smiled at her.

'I'd like to help' she said.

'No, absolutely not. You just read' he said in the manner of 'Don't you dirty your pretty crinolines and your perfect dainty little hands and just carry on embroidering your cushions.'

'I can read later, I want to help.'

She leaned forward and stared into his eyes. He looked uncomfortable which was the result she was after. He closed his eyes for a moment – and you could almost feel him giving in. Come on Ned, you chauvinistic...

' All right then. I suppose many hands make light work. You'll need boots.'

'If I can fight my way through to the garage, my walking boots are in my car boot.'

'With the depth of the snow out there, you might be better with wellies. My sister's are on the boot rack in the broom cupboard.'

Bridie pulled a face at wearing someone else's smelly wellies. Ned noticed and he looked sternly at her.

'If you can wear my sister's knickers you can wear her wellies' he said, leaving Bridie embarrassed and Mrs H with a smile on her face.

Chapter 11

Still December 23rd

During her extensive research into the building and lands of Midwinter Hall, looking for ownership of that stupid field, Bridie had become an expert on geographical trivia. For example, the name 'Wolds' originally came from the Old English word 'wald', meaning forest. More specifically in this case, gently rolling hills once covered by ancient woodland.

This was why the 'top field' was at the top of a gently rising slope for Ned and why it was known as the 'bottom field' by Zinnia. If these names had been used in any documents it would have made identification easier. As it was, it was known as 'Land area, 1.89 acres, to the North' which was no help to anybody.

Henry and Rose's cottage was built originally for farm workers on the land. It was at the bottom of another gentle slope to the left of Midwinter Hall as you faced it. The track led away from the last of the greenhouses towards a flat area of land. On it stood a red brick cottage with a pantiled roof and chimney. It had a small cottage garden and an allotment garden, neither of which could be seen at the moment underneath the snow. Nor could the track for that matter.

Bridie and Ned crossed over to the last glass house in their wellies, lifting their legs up in a passable imitation of the Greek Presidential Guards with their high-stepping march. They waited, shovels in hands, for Marcus to fetch the mini-digger. They heard it rumbling and stepped back from where they thought the track was.

He was taking the top layer of snow off, which judging by a white column standing frozen on top of a wheelbarrow, was a least a foot deep or more. They would then take their shovels and try to get down to the ground below. If they left any compacted snow on it, Henry and Rose would effectively be stuck in their home if it iced over.

'I'm going to tarmac this track' Ned grumbled to himself. 'It's not safe for them'

'As if snow wouldn't have fallen on the tarmac, just the same?'

Ned glowered at her.

The dogs had come along to 'help', which mostly involved Tamsin rounding Tink up, to stop her getting shovelled up either by the two hand shovels or by the big mechanical scoop of the digger. The digger's engine suddenly slowed to a hum as Tam's barks became frenzied. Bridie looked up to see Tink standing in the scooped-up snow of the digger's bucket - a few feet off the ground - and looking as if it was the best fairground ride in the world.

Ned tutted and went to pick her up as he and Marcus exchanged grins. Tam fussed around her now she was back on the ground. It was the nearest Bridie had seen the normally calm sheepdog display panic, as she really loved her naughty little sidekick, as a parent would with a wayward toddler.

The rest of the time passed without incident. Marcus had stopped the digger outside Rose Cottage, its name painted on a wooden sign on the door by Henry for his wife. He unloaded the big bag of food from the cab and two large sacks of wood that were tied to the back. He had a quick word with Henry, then emptied a load of rock salt into the trough to scatter on the way back. He was going to continue the snow clearing all the way to the door of the hall.

Bridie couldn't believe she was sweating. The temperature was below freezing and she was getting too warm. By the time they reached the door of the cottage, she was exhausted, although she straightened up and smiled happily when Ned looked across at her. She wouldn't let him see any weakness.

There was a patch in front of the door which was already cleared and salted by Henry, who stood there holding his hand out to Ned.

'Well done, lad' he said shaking his hand and forgoing any name formalities, 'and you too, lass. I'll be able to go up and check the greenhouses now.'

'You will not' replied Ned. 'I can do that on my way back.'

Henry looked disappointed.

'I suppose if you're doing it today then... I'll be there in the morning though.'

'It's Christmas Eve tomorrow.' Ned raised his eyes heavenward.

'Them seedlings don't know that' laughed Henry. He would be there tomorrow if he could, they all knew that.

Rose, apple-cheeked and with a broad smile, called out to them.

'Come on in and get warm. I've got a pot of tea and some spice cake and cheese waiting.'

Bridie grinned. This was a Yorkshire thing. When she first came here, the thought of eating Wensleydale cheese with sweet Christmas cake seemed most strange. However, once she tried it, it seemed the perfect pairing.

*

It was cosy and warm in the little living room with its well-worn settee and chairs, covered with hand-knitted blankets in earth colours and homemade patchwork cushions. The wood burner was kicking out plenty of heat and they all sat around it, their faces glowing in the firelight.

It was obvious to Bridie watching his interaction with Henry that Ned thought the world of him, almost like a father figure perhaps. He must have been fairly young when his father died. Twenty? Twenty-one? And he had not been in the best of health anyway for a few years before that. Sir Albert – or Bertie as he was always known - had never really recovered from a nasty fall from a temperamental horse.

Again this made Bridie think of her own father, a lovely man and very kind and generous to whoever he was working to help at the time - but not very generous with his presence for his own daughter. She wondered if that's why she got on so well with Henry herself.

Rose could almost but not quite rival Mrs H with her baking. She pressed more cake and cheese on them both and then some homemade flapjacks from a tin with Paddington Bear on the front. Bridie had to refuse the second flapjack in case she couldn't make it back up the slope with the extra weight and Ned would have to put a rope around her wrists and drag her bodily behind him. She had drifted off into an X-rated fantasy about this scene when Ned shook her shoulder as he handed her coat to her.

'Penny for them' he said.

'They're worth far more than that' she grinned at him.

He looked puzzled, which seemed to be his default expression whenever he looked at Bridie. They all hugged and Ned turned at the door.

'If that fuel doesn't arrive in the morning, we'll bring some more wood down.'

Bridie frowned.

'If it doesn't - and I doubt it will - what will you do about cooking Christmas dinner? You've only got the Range oven for cooking apart from the one ring on the wood burner. Do you come up to the hall anyway?'

Henry seemed embarrassed.

'We just tend to celebrate here quietly with a chicken dinner and all the trimmings. I have a bottle of beer and Rose has a glass of sherry. Maybe a glass of homemade wine or two. We're not ones for celebrating much.'

Bridie looked at Ned with meaning. He misinterpreted.

'Mrs H will cook something and we can bring it down for you.' he said.

Bridie stared at him with even more meaning. She couldn't - in her eyes - have made it clearer if she had written it on a placard and held it up in front of him.

INVITE THEM TO THE HALL FOR CHRISTMAS DAY!

He looked so puzzled this time that she almost felt sorry for him, then–

'Not to worry' he said, 'I'm sure the delivery will be here - they deliver till noon on Christmas Eve. No more snow forecast and anyway we have to get Bridie home to celebrate *her* Christmas.'

Woop-de-woo!, thought Bridie, you don't know how sad my Christmases are, Sir Edward Fynch-Stratton.

'I'll phone the emergency services up if you like and order an airlift out of here, as you're so keen to be rid of me' she said in a pathetic voice looking hurt at the same time, a la Puss in Boots from Shrek.

'Oh God, I didn't mean that. I don't *want* you to go. W-w-what I mean is, I don't want you to go if you don't want to go. If you get stuck here, is what I'm trying to say.'

He tailed off, looking uncomfortable and confused.

'That's okay. I understand' she whispered raising her eyes up to his with an abandoned puppy expression.

His eyes narrowed and you could see the penny drop as he realised she'd been playing him like a violin. He looked like he was going to say something but thought better of it.

'Let's wait and see what tomorrow brings' he said as pleasantly as he could manage and then walked out of the door.

Henry and Rose who were way ahead of Ned in the penny-dropping stakes, started laughing quietly while Bridie winked at them.

'Poor lad. You shouldn't tease him' said Henry, still laughing.

'What - and spoil my fun?' beamed Bridie and set off after Ned who was almost halfway towards the greenhouses.

Chapter 12

A Suggestion

'Rain's forecast overnight, it could wash the snow away' said Mrs H doubtfully as the radio switched smoothly from the weather forecast to 'I'm dreaming of a White Christmas' without a hint of irony.

'I've heard that before' replied Bridie. 'Yesterday, in fact, when they first forecast rain that would wash the snow away...'

'Henry says there's more snow on the way' intoned Marcus, as he wiped his feet on the doormat. He had just caught the tail end of the conversation.

'Now. I'd rather believe Henry any day over that lot at the Met Office. He goes by nature, pine cones, the ring around the moon, clouds in the sky, behaviour of animals...', Mrs

H tailed off 'Been right more times than the BBC that's for sure.'

'That means I might be stuck here tomorrow too' frowned Bridie, although in truth it wouldn't be much hardship for her.

'Nothing spoiling is there? You said your family aren't in England. What would you normally be doing?'

'My best friend Chantal has invited me over but I wouldn't get there in this weather anyway. My phone's reception is terrible at the moment but I used the library laptop yesterday. Chantal – she's half French - had sent a panicked email one hour before saying they're snowed in too and not to attempt to get over.'

Bridie remembered the actual words were–

'I've been trying to phone you but can't get through. PLEASE let me know you're okay!!!'

Then–

'Don't even ATTEMPT to come over here for Xmas if it's still like this! Our village is COMPLETELY cut off!! I'm guessing your place is too? The whole world has gone white! Beautiful to look at unless you want to travel in it.

We will get together when it's gone. New Year maybe? Fingers crossed!!!

***DON'T FORGET** to let me know you're okay – ASAP!*
Lots of snowy love
Chantal xxx'

'There you are you see, it's fate' smiled Mrs H, 'It'll be nice to have a bit of company for Christmas.'

Bridie thought of Henry and Rose spending their Christmases quietly at home. She thought of Mrs H eating her turkey and sprouts in the kitchen while Ned carried his through on a tray to his office, or maybe even the dining room in solitary splendour as it was a special occasion. She thought of Marcus collecting his festive feast from the back door on a plate covered in foil to keep it warm - and going back to his flat above the stables to eat it by himself, as he always did. As Bridie usually did. As Zinnia Pelham did - no husband, no family, on her own and cut off for Christmas.

It was just one day. That's what everyone said and that was true. You could ignore Christmas. Treat it as something to get over and done with. The commercial money-grabbing, false bonhomie of the modern Christmas had made the 'It's just one day' concept a lot easier to bear.

Yet, not too long ago, Christmas always meant family gatherings whether you were poor or rich. It meant dancing, singing, playing games. It meant eating festive fayre, whether it was one of the chickens you kept in your back garden along with the vegetables you grew there that were in season - or for the more well-off, goose and later turkey.

For both rich and poor, rooms were decorated with evergreens and candles to light the darkness, The coming together of family and friends, the provision of comfort and warmth in a cold and inhospitable world. The one time a year that everybody greeted even strangers, with good wishes for a Happy Christmas. They exchanged small, homemade presents, or elaborate shop-bought gifts, according to their circumstances. Christmas brought light into their lives.

Bridie took a deep breath now.

'Here's a radical thought. Why don't we all celebrate Christmas together?'

*

Ned had chosen the moment that she voiced her radical thought, to enter the kitchen. Instead of a follow-on conversation, there was a follow-on silence. Mrs H turned to the oven to get the gingerbread out. Even the enticing spicy smell couldn't distract Bridie from her mission.

'I might not even be here' she said pointedly. 'I might have been airlifted out by Christmas Day - but not the rest of you. I know it's only one day but it's the one day where you *can* all get together, eat together and have a drink with each other.'

She looked round appealing silently for backup from at least one of them but Mrs H was busy putting the gingerbread on a cooling rack and was concentrating suspiciously hard on the task. Marcus glanced between Bridie and Ned, then mumbled something about 'getting back.' Even the dogs looked at each other as if they knew trouble was brewing. Finally, Ned spoke up.

'I understand why you're trying to do this. The spirit of Christmas and all that - but it's just how we do things now. It's how we all like it.'

'How'd you know? Have you asked them?'

'Really Bridie, I don't think it's any of your business what we do on Christmas day. You're not normally here.'

She blinked at him but didn't say anything which made Ned look uncomfortable. He went on.

'I can't understand why you're so adamant about it. Only last week you were saying that you didn't really want to go to your friend's and would prefer to spend it on your own.'

Bridie looked down, defeated.

'I did, didn't I? In my defence, my friend has enough on her plate without me.'

She stepped back and sidled past him.

'Bridie,' he called to her. 'I'm sorry but life isn't like it is in Christmas films you know....'

He looked awkward and it was mirrored in Bridie's expression.

'I do know and I'm sorry. I shouldn't have interfered, it *isn't* my business. I just thought it would be nice for once - for me too. I think I must be some sort of a control freak, trying to organise everyone into doing what I want and not what they want. Sorry again.'

There was no doubting her sincerity. He gave a wobbly sort of smile and held his hand out.

'Truce?' he said kindly.

'Truce' she smiled and grasped his hand.

A surge of electricity went through her body which had nothing to do with static and everything to do with the expression in those gentle and forgiving blue eyes.

*

Bridie ran her eyes along one of the shelves in the study. She was looking for a book to read but her mind was still focused on the earlier conversation. Honestly, she thought, I'm an uninvited guest in my boss's house, imprisoned here through no fault of his - and he had to listen to her berating him on his Christmas routine, in his own home. Her cheeks felt hot, as his puzzled expression came back to her. She was trying to keep out of his way now. He was in his office, still hoping to find the mythical document.

She wondered whether he had felt anything when he shook her hand. It was probably just static anyway, but why did her heart miss a beat when she thought of him gazing down at her? She picked up a book at random and laughed at the gods of irony. 'Christmas Customs Through the Ages.' Well, she might as well use it as a stick to beat herself with, so she would learn her lesson. She took it over to the window seat to make the most of the fading light and then frowned. Why was this book on the shelves of someone who didn't care about Christmas?

*

In his office Ned sat with a cardboard file in his hand, unopened, as he stared into space. He was thinking of the touch of her hand, her green eyes and her red hair tumbling down around her shoulders. He shook his head and made another attempt to get interested in the top field.

Chapter 13

Christmas Eve morning

The sounds of a house coming to life drifted up to Bridie, who had just woken and was still dozy. What were people doing up in the middle of the night? It was pitch black.

She staggered over to the window and drew back the thick brocade curtains. Rubbing her eyes, she tried to see through the fog of sleep then realised she couldn't see because there was a blizzard going on outside the window.

Snow was being blown one way and then the other, diagonally and horizontally. Already resigned to her fate from before she went to sleep, she made her way to the bathroom.

She emerged refreshed with squeaky clean hair. This would no doubt settle into a red fluffy cloud around her face, without her special hair dryer. She picked out yet more of her clothes buddy's outfits from the wardrobe. Black skinny jeans and an oatmeal slouchy jumper. She pulled out a long black woollen scarf too, which she would need later. She folded the bottoms of the trousers over to make turn-ups but she quite liked the length of the jumper. It made her feel quite snuggly until she looked out of the window again.

Snow was still falling but just vertically now in a much less frantic way. The scene revealed to her was bleak, if beautiful. Snow covered all the paths and the driveway that Marcus had already cleared. Virgin snow was everywhere. No doggie paw prints or human footprints to be seen at the front of the hall.

She heard a whimpering and shuffling at the other side of her bedroom door. She opened it to reveal a honey brown bundle, cocking her head to one side as if to say 'why aren't you downstairs yet?'

'All right Tink, I'm coming' she said, bending down to rub her soft fur until the little dog hared off along the landing and down the stairs. Bridie caught the smell of frying and followed it. Waiting at the bottom of the stairs, always the more mature and sensible of the dynamic duo, was Tam, waiting to be made of fuss of too. Bridie very happily obliged.

It was lovely being greeted by dogs on a morning, she thought. She had never had one, with moving around so much but if she decided to settle around this area permanently, a dog was definitely on the cards.

'That smells good' she said, entering the kitchen and going over to Mrs H to give her a quick hug.

Funny how being thrown into a hostage situation made you feel closer to people who were only workmates the week before, although Mrs H had always been a favourite.

Bridie briefly wished she could have found little presents for them all. Normally, a last-minute Amazon delivery would have been great but they wouldn't make it in this weather and if they did that meant she could go home so… Anyway, knowing her luck she would get one of those delivery drivers who was on a tight schedule. They would knock for all of 5 seconds while you did a Usain bolt down the hallway to catch him. By that time he would already have strapped his cross-country skis on and be back at his van pretending not to notice you as you wave your arms at him like a windmill in a gale.

'There's a plate here with your name on it' said Mrs H. 'I was just about to put it in the warming oven but you can sit down now and eat. You'll need a good hot meal inside you in this weather.'

You see, thought Bridie, that's what a *proper* mother would say, but they probably only existed in Ladybird books and 1950s films. She took a mouthful of fried bread guiltily, she must stop putting her parents down. Just because they weren't the archetypical, nurturing parents didn't mean that they were bad people. They most definitely weren't. All right, she was left to her own devices more often than not but it had made her the independent, confident person she now was. There were a hell of a lot worse parents in the world and she *was* loved. In their own unique way, they *did* love her. She would go over again in the summer and help out at the Tribal Displacement camp again. There were people who needed her parents far more than she did.

'Aren't you eating, Mrs H? Or anyone else?' she asked, dipping the hash browns into the perfectly runny egg.

'I had mine an hour ago. The men have had theirs and are going to try and clear the paths again. You just missed them.'

Bridie couldn't help being glad about this. She didn't fancy facing Ned and his breakfast tray this early in the morning. She looked at the clock. It was 6:45 a.m. She still felt bad.

'Was he - Ned, I mean, was he okay this morning?'

What she really meant was 'Do you think he's forgiven me?' Mrs H cast a glance over her shoulder, then put the pans to one side as she came to sit down beside Bridie. She reached for the cups and poured them both a hot, steaming cup of tea, pushing one across to Bridie. She looked her straight in the eye.

'You must have wondered what was going on yesterday? Regarding Christmas, that is?'

'I think I got the message. In the words of Alan Rickman as the Sheriff of Nottingham - Christmas is cancelled. I'll sit with you in the kitchen like a good girl. It certainly seems like I won't be going anywhere else.'

Mrs H put her head down. Then her shoulders rose and fell and she seemed to come to a decision. She took a sip of tea.

'It's a bit more complicated than that. I shouldn't really be telling you this as I feel disloyal.'

'Don't tell me if it makes you feel uncomfortable.' Bridie said quickly.

'No, I think Ned felt bad about it himself last night and unless things change drastically, you'll be here with us for Christmas. So you deserve to know why Ned doesn't celebrate Christmas.'

'I shouldn't have said anything, sticking my nose in again. I've always been outspoken but I'm going to have to rein back.'

'I have to say' began Mrs H, 'that it was a nice idea for us all to spend Christmas together.'

'Really?' Bridie was surprised.

'And under different circumstances, we would all probably enjoy that. Well, I *know* we would because we've talked about it.'

'Really?!' Bridie repeated in parrot fashion.

'But we couldn't because of Ned.'

Bridie frowned but kept quiet as she felt it was needed and she leaned forward to hear the story.

Chapter 14

Christmas Eve Revelations

'I'm not telling you much, only the basics because if anyone tells that story, it should be Ned. Eight years ago tomorrow, Ned's father, Sir Albert, died in this house.'

'Not in the bedroom I'm sleeping in?' Bridie pulled a face. So did Mrs H, an exasperated one.

'Are you going to listen?'

'Yes sorry... but–'

'No, not in that room. The one next to it. Now, I've told you he'd been ill for a while. The fall from the horse, besides injuring his back gave him a nasty knock on the head and after that, well, you never knew which Bertie you were getting. The kind and funny man you had before - or the one with a short fuse who could lose his temper with you over nothing and the reason for it was inside his head.

'Although Ned knew this, the outbursts upset him. He understood that his father couldn't help himself but as Ned bore the brunt of most of his temper - Elise, his sister was married and lived away - it was hard for him to bear.

'This particular Christmas Day morning, Ned had taken his breakfast up on a tray as Bertie rarely got out of bed towards the end. I don't know exactly what happened but five minutes later Ned came down and slammed the tray on this table, the contents uneaten and his present to his father still on the tray, unopened. He stormed out and went for a walk. Probably to the wood.

'He came back a while later, racing through the front door like the Hounds of Lucifer were after him. I was in the hall talking to Elise who had come with her husband and son for Christmas Day. He looked at us wild-eyed, shouted 'Send for the doctor. Now!', and shot up the stairs to his father's bedroom.

'His sister followed him while I rang the doctor, though in truth I didn't know what to tell him. I just said it was an emergency at Midwinter Hall and to get here as soon as he could. In the event, he was too late but apparently, there was nothing he could have done to save him anyway. He'd had a brain aneurysm which had been threatening for a long time.

'Luckily Ned and his sister had the last twenty minutes of his life with him. According to his sister, Ned made his peace with his father before he went, which is good but....'

'Christmas has bad memories?'

'Yes, exactly. For the first few years, he shut himself away. On Christmas Day I used to knock and take him his Christmas dinner, but it came back virtually untouched as if he shouldn't be enjoying food or well, anything, on the day his father died.

'He's much better now than he was, but I had to let you know that he's not just being a killjoy. There is a reason for him not celebrating Christmas. It's understandable. Don't you think?'

'Oh, I do understand now. Completely. Thank you for telling me.' Bridie replied and stared out of the window, 'but don't you think it would do him good to put those memories behind him and make more pleasant ones?'

'Well! I just give up!' said Mrs H, throwing her hands up in the air. 'You're not going to let it drop are you?'

Bridie looked suitably chastened.

' I suppose I'd better, hadn't I?'

Mrs H smiled kindly at her.

'I know you're doing it for his own good - and for ours, as it would be nice to at least eat dinner all together. It doesn't matter if you or I think it would be good for him though, it has to be *his* decision. Do you see?'

'Yes, my lovely Mrs H' smiled Bridie, getting up and giving her a hug which had the older woman beaming. 'I promise you I'll keep schtum. At least you and I can eat dinner together. Now, let me help. I won't get in your way, I promise' she added noticing Mrs H's raised eyebrows.

*

From his place in the hallway where he'd been standing with his empty coffee mug unable to move, Ned crept silently back to the sitting room. He'd been stuck for the entire conversation, unable to walk either into the kitchen where he would embarrass them or back to the room in case they heard him. It was only when the pans started clattering and the tap was turned on that he felt safe to move.

He didn't know how long he sat on the settee, deep in thought until he realised he was still holding the mug. Taking a deep breath, he left it on the coffee table and went out of the front door.

*

An hour later after a piece of pork pie and a slice of Stollen cake in the study, Bridie was ready to go back to work in the kitchen again. She was enjoying the Christmas preparations. It reminded her of helping her Nanna out when she stayed there. She remembered baking some gingerbread men and women with hats and Santa suits iced onto them. They had been far from perfect but *she* had made them and her grandparents loved them - or so they said. She smiled to herself as she put the book back.

She had been reading the 'Christmas Customs' book again. There were some good ideas, old-fashioned but nothing wrong with that. It occurred to her that it must have been Ned's father's study as Ned himself hardly used it. That led her to wonder if the Fynch-Stratton family used the book when Ned had been young, before their mother died - and if they had fun family Christmases then.

'They're waiting for you' said Mrs H as Bridie walked into the kitchen.

'Who's waiting for me?' asked Bridie, puzzled, until Mrs H nodded towards a large cooling rack on the table, where twelve naked gingerbread men lay. She laughed and putting her arm around Mrs H's shoulders, gave her another spontaneous hug which had the housekeeper, head cook and bottle washer, grinning from ear to ear.

'They've turned out perfectly, haven't they?' she told Bridie, 'your Nanna taught you well.'

'She did' smiled Bridie 'but they'd be a bit cold in this weather. I'd better put some clothes on them quickly.'

Mrs H handed over the icing sugar, food colourings and a piping bag. Bridie looked shocked as she had only ever seen the ready-made icing in supermarkets. She remembered now, her Nanna spooning soft icing into a cotton bag with a nozzle on the end, just like these. In for a penny, in for a pound, she thought and listened to Mrs H's instructions for the perfect consistency of icing.

After another hour or so of dusting mince pies with icing sugar, stirring the gravy which would be added to the meat juices tomorrow and peeling countless carrots and potatoes, she looked up to see Tam and Tink sitting at her feet, staring at her expectantly.

'What have I done?' she asked.

'Nothing. I think they're looking to you to take them for a walk.'

'In this? Tink will get as far as the threshold, dip her dainty little paw in and then scuttle back inside.'

'Yet, there they both are' laughed Mrs H, indicating the dogs, who had both started doing a little dance with their front paws while shuffling their bottoms from side to side.

'Oh God, all right, come on' she laughed 'before it gets dark.'

The dog darted to the front door and Bridie frowned. 'I thought they'd be out with Ned. Where is he? I haven't seen him once today.'

'They went with him to the greenhouses first thing but then he walked the land, checking it all on Bessie. I think he'll be out shovelling the snow again down to Henry's after Marcus cleared it with the digger.'

Bridie had heard Marcus clearing the path again while she was in the study. She had wanted to run out and ask him why he was shovelling snow in a blizzard but she didn't think it would be appreciated. Besides the wind had dropped and the snow was only falling softly now.

'He didn't ask me if I'd help this time' Bridie said, sounding petulant even to her own ears.

'He said the snow wasn't as compacted as last time. Anyway, I said I needed your help here. Was that okay?'

Bridie thought of the lovely day she'd spent with this homely caring woman, in a warm cosy inviting kitchen with a million different aromas invading her senses.

'It was more than okay. I've loved my day with you. I'll take the dogs up to the wood. The holly grove, not the other one.'

Mrs H. glanced at her giving her a funny little look that Bridie couldn't interpret. Something came to the forefront of Bridie's memory.

'You said that Ned went to the wood just before his father died?' she asked.

Mrs H. looked defensive.

'Did I? Well yes, he did - probably.'

' The ancient wood? The Silent Wood?

The older woman's head shot up but she answered quietly.

'Yes'

'Mrs H, You know the Rushtons?'

'Just over the ridge at the far side of the wood? Course I do. Been here almost as long as the Fynch's have.'

'There's a teenage granddaughter...'

' Leyla?'

'Is there only one? About eighteen?'

'That'll be her. There are much younger ones too. What about her?'

'What does she look like?' asked Bridie in a low voice.

'Oh, well, in the last few years, she's put a bit of weight on which isn't good on a five-foot-nothing frame. Erm, mousey-brown short hair, cut as short as a man's at the back – shaved really. Broad shoulders, always wears those horn-rimmed glasses...? Bridie?'

Mrs H watched, bewildered while the dogs raced to catch Bridie up as she was already at the door and putting her coat on.

Chapter 15

Christmas Eve – The Meeting

The snow was softer to wade through than before but that didn't stop Tink from disappearing as soon as she reached the front lawn, Bridie bent down to pick her up and the little dog turned to her with a disgruntled look and with a dollop of snow on her nose.

Bridie laughed and thought that she might just as well have carried her outside the front door, set her down to make a yellow puddle in the snow, and then stood with her for 10 minutes. She wasn't going to get much exercise this way. The problem was that Tink didn't want her good friend Tam having all the fun and would tag along anyway out of sheer cussedness.

Tamsin was bouncing ahead like a space-hopper, trying to keep as snow-free as possible under her belly. They soon joined onto the track that led to the two woods and as trees sheltered it to either side, the snow wasn't as thick here, so she put a reluctant Tink down. She grinned as she watched her pick her ladylike way forward, front paws raised alternately in the air like a dressage-dog. Very soon, they were surrounded by thick woods on either side.

Bridie thought back to the conversation with Ned. When she had asked about Derry, she had described the girl as pretty and slim - and Ned who seemed to have known the family very well said it was probably the granddaughter, whom he knew was the opposite to her description – and whom he knew wasn't called Derry, or something that sounded like it.

Combine this with the fact he obviously used the wood as a place of solace when he was younger, although he said he hardly went there, and it all added up to him hiding something.

The eerily-lit tree, the glowing dress, the unusual voice and accent... Everything now seemed stranger than she had thought when it could have just been an eccentric teenager in fancy dress, possibly high on something and definitely quite mad. Was there something eerie about the wood as Zinnia had said, something sacred? And what about the dogs' reluctance to go in and Fred's reluctance to be near it?

She felt a compulsion to visit the place again and either put the supernatural theory that was jumping around her head now to bed or - or what?

She had reached the place where the central path led off to the right to the newer oak and holly wood - and to the left, to the Silent Wood. Tam sat down at the edge taking up her observation post and stared down into the ancient oak wood. Tink put a foot forward, registered that she would be sitting on snow, and looked up at Bridie imploringly.

'All right, come on' she grinned, as she picked her up and deposited her just inside the holly grove where the taller oaks offered more protection from the elements. The snow was still falling gently but constantly. She called Tam over to keep Tink company. The dog moved reluctantly but as soon as she realised she could see straight down the path ahead leading through the opposite wood, which Bridie would be taking, she settled down quietly. My guardians, thought Bridie and gave them both an extra hug.

'I won't be long, stay there' she said but she knew they would.

Bridie walked through the woods reverently trying not to make any noise or disturb anything. This was the effect it had on you. She looked up as she moved forward slowly. The old oak branches arched over far above her, creating a tunnel through which she could glimpse an indigo sky, heavy with snowfall yet to come. Day was giving way to dusk and soon night would fall. Tonight the moon was shining brightly but she could only catch a glimpse of it through the branches as the snow filtered down, sending a powdery coating onto her hat and coat.

She walked for a while keeping watch for the larger oak tree on the right. The one she had seen a few days ago. She went further and further - surely she must see it soon -but when she turned back she could only just make out Tam as a speck on the horizon and Tink couldn't be seen at all by the human eye. She must have passed it. Surely not? Its size alone made it stand out amongst the other huge trees around it. There had been no ethereal glow either, but she still wasn't sure if that had been the girl's dress.

She felt stupidly disappointed. She looked towards the other end of the wood and saw no glow, or any oak that stood out from the others. Well, that was that. She had been tempted over to the 'dark side' where she had never strayed before and obviously, her original feelings were the ones she should stick to. Superstition had its place but that place wasn't on her radar anymore. She had heard of phosphorescence emanating from trees in the shadows. This was the obvious, scientific explanation.

She liked the old folklore tales, but they were nothing more than stories. Told around a fire long ago to entertain people who didn't have books, TV and the internet to keep them occupied. She laughed at her earlier feelings. She was letting this place get to her, this place - and its people. She turned to go back to Midwinter Hall when she had a sudden thought.

If it *was* a guest of the Rushton family that she had seen, they were making their way to their farmhouse through the woods. She wondered how far away the farm was. Out of curiosity, she turned to face the direction in which Derry had pointed and without any forethought - or thought at all, which was normal for her anyway - she plunged into the dense woodland.

She caught glimpses of the start of a fiery sunset, between the more spindly oak trees. It was the former indigo, striped with an unnatural yellow, bright like the yellow of a rainbow. She continued for a while until a lighter sky showed that the trees were thinning out. She arrived at the edge of the wood to see the whole, beautiful sky displayed above her. Black, dark blue, purple, yellow with hints of orange. It looked like something Van Gogh would paint. She was transfixed, taking it all in as though Nature had put on this display just for her. It felt personal.

She knew this though - she had never looked at Nature, the sky, the trees, even the snow in quite the same way as she had since she started working at Midwinter Hall. It was as if it was working some sort of magic on this previously non-emotional, practical person that was Bridie Emms. She felt elated, euphoric - and she liked feeling this way.

Perhaps she *should* open her heart and soul to the wonders of Nature. It certainly felt better than the relatively drab existence that she'd had these last few years. Magical was a good word for the transformation that was happening to her. An epiphany perhaps.

Casting her eyes over the countryside, almost in darkness now, she saw that the nearest building - the light shining in its windows - was quite a way away in the distance. Too far for a girl in a flimsy dress to walk to in snow, surely? The sky started losing its colours and she realised she had to get back to the dogs and to the Hall.

As she turned, the wood was scarily dark, disorientating her. Which direction should she go? Why hadn't she brought her phone with her? Her breathing started to come faster. She wasn't one to panic but...

There, suddenly, in the distance, there was a glow. A greeny-yellow glow. Her heartbeat quickened because she knew what it was. She made her way towards it - a beacon in the night.

Chapter 16

A Conversation?

As Bridie reached the glow, she noticed that suddenly, the widest, tallest tree that she had seen before was now somehow in the middle of the wood, emitting light as it had on the Midwinter Solstice.

Trees don't move, do they? Bridie put the thoughts out of her head, as visions of the walking trees from Lord of the Rings marching towards her, crowded her mind. There was no doubt it was the same tree. It had a particular shape. Its branches were in the shape of a giant umbrella and in the summer, its canopy would provide shelter and safety underneath.

She stared up at it and noticed that the branches weren't touching the trees on either side, as though the other trees had made room for it. She brought her eyes downwards.

She put her hands against the trunk. It would need two or maybe three people holding hands to reach completely around its girth. She sighed and felt that the tree sighed too, its light dimming. Suddenly there was a warmth across her shoulders and down her back and she turned. There, smiling serenely at her was Derry, with a glow around that seemed as though it had transferred from the tree to the girl.

Or was it a girl? She was wearing a dark cloak over a gently glowing white gown and - she wasn't a girl anymore. She was a woman around the same age as Bridie but recognizably the same person. Bridie's voice wouldn't work. It stuck in her throat. When it did come out, the words were both croaky and ridiculous.

'Merry Christmas Eve' she rasped.

The lady smiled as though it was a private joke.

'Blessed Yule to you' she said in that strange unrecognisable accent. Her voice was multi-tonal. It sounded like a bell, a whisper, a breeze passing through leaves.

They looked at each other, Bridie smiling like someone from Wallace and Gromit.

Eventually, she broke the silence and because she didn't know what else to say, she said,

'I'd better get back to the dogs.'

' They are waiting patiently' Derry said.

Bridie went to walk past her, apprehensive in case she was taken up by Derry into the oak tree's aura and never seen again. She gritted her teeth. You're an idiot, she thought and then turned around.

'How come you can speak to me if–' she could hardly believe she was saying this, 'if you're some sort of spirit of the woods?'

'Am I?'

'The spirit of the woods?'

'Speaking to you?'

It was then with a shock that made her feet, hands and brain tingle, that she realised that this lady before her - and the girl at the midsummer solstice - had not moved their lips except to smile or laugh. Their words, or thoughts, must have gone straight to Bridie's consciousness. She gasped and later, Bridie would realise that, despite all the evidence building up until now, it was at this point when she had to give way to a belief in the supernatural.

'Will I see you again?' she whispered.

'Within the twelve days.'

This time, Bridie watched the tranquil face, gazing at her intently. Her lips had not moved.

'I have to go. Blessed Yule' she said, self-consciously.

They smiled at each other and she felt a strange sort of kinship with this spirit, entity, ghost or whatever she was. She felt happy in her presence, if a little awestruck.

With great reluctance, she tore herself away. If she hadn't been worried about the dogs, she might have stayed there forever - which was ultimately a worrying thought. As she moved further away she kept glancing back. She lost sight of Derry fairly quickly, but there was a faint glow from the giant oak which lasted until she was safely on the path and on her way to Tam and Tink

*

Ned was standing on the steps, the collar turned up on his long, khaki woollen coat. He didn't look in her direction. The dogs went ahead but sensed his mood and just sat at his feet instead of making a fuss of him. Without addressing Bridie, he stood back a couple of paces into the hallway and shouted.

'She's back Mrs H, in one piece, apparently.' Mrs H bustled out of the kitchen.

'Thank goodness for that. We were worried about you. You shot out of here like a bat out of hell and when it got dark, well...' she said, managing to look aggrieved and thankful at the same time. 'as long as you're okay.'

Bridie stepped into the hallway dripping melted snow over the floor.

'I'm really sorry, Mrs H. I didn't realise how dark it was getting and so quickly too. I'll be in soon to give you a hand if you forgive me?'

Mrs H gave her an exasperated look but then smiled showing deep dimples in her chubby cheeks.

'Go and get yourself changed out of those damp clothes and I'll see you later' she said before returning to the warmth of the kitchen.

Bridie looked back to see Ned had moved away from the doorway. Tink had sensibly followed Mrs H through to the kitchen but Tam must have gone with him. She ran back outside to see them both heading in the direction of the stables and ran to catch them up.

'Where are you going? Can I come with you?' she asked breathlessly, sounding like a six-year-old child.

'I'm going to see Bessie. Go back inside' he said shortly.

Why was he so annoyed with her? She didn't understand. Although Mrs H had said *we* were worried about you. She caught him up and walked by his side, looking up at him. She could tell he was annoyed, which made her stare even more intensely. The abandoned puppy dog look was going to be her next move but he gave in before that.

'What?' he said.

'What do you mean 'What'?' she asked innocently.

'You've got something on your mind and you're desperate to tell me. Spit it out, woman.'

She was starting to get annoyed herself now but she bit it back. She had lots of questions but dare she say anything when he was in this mood? She would have to be very sensitive to do so. Very tactful.

'Why did you lie to me?' she did indeed spit it out, about as far from tactful as she could get.

'Jesus Christ almighty.' He stopped dead. 'You disappear - with MY DOGS, I might add - in thick snow. In the dark. Not taking either a torch or your phone, which was still on the kitchen table - and somehow you manage to turn it round to be *my* fault!'

He ran his fingers through his hair in exasperation. He had given her a dressing down before but somehow this time, she knew it was because he cared and not because he was truly angry with her. Unfortunately, this didn't translate into the compassionate reply it should have.

'Don't you take the moral high ground, Ned. You know you lied to me about the Rushton's granddaughter.'

He looked like he didn't know how to deal with this and instead started walking slowly towards the stables. After a moment or two, he spoke.

'You've been to the old oak wood then?'

' I have.'

Silence again, then.

'And did you meet any strange women in fancy dress again?'

'Did you?' she said before she could prevent it from spilling out, 'on the night your father died?'

It was a toss-up between who looked the most shocked. Ned because of 'how dare she?' and Bridie because, well, how could she be so bloody thoughtless? What did it matter and what business was it of hers anyway? It was because he lied about the granddaughter but, so what? Did he really deserve this?

'Oh God, I'm so sorry. I don't know why I said that. Please ignore me and please forgive me. I was just annoyed when you said that you thought the girl I met might have been the granddaughter when it patently wasn't. You've seen her before though. The same girl I met.'

He was staring into the distance in the direction of the Silent Wood.

'You're wrong' he said quietly. 'I haven't seen this girl you mentioned.'

Bridie was crestfallen. She'd been so sure. She wished the ground, snow and all, would open and swallow her up. Anything to get away from Ned's intense displeasure and her own embarrassment.

Chapter 17

The Summons

Bessie was standing there looking snug and warm within the thick stone walls of the stable. She had plenty of hay in the hay basket and lots of straw on the floor. She whinnied and looked so pleased to see Ned that it looked like she would jump over the gate. The old horse was happy to see Bridie too, as she made time to call in and see her every day to make a fuss of her. Ned looked surprised.

'I'm a regular visitor.' she explained. They had walked up to the stable silently, Bridie zipping her mouth for once.

'I hear you surveyed your estate with Bessie earlier?'

'Yes, it gets her out for a bit of exercise- and it's the easiest way of doing it. Quad bikes are all right in their place but they churn the ground up much more than Bessie here. You can't beat the old ways.' he said sounding as though he were in his nineties. He felt in his pockets and brought out some of the oat, apple and carrot treats, baked especially for Bessie by Mrs H.

'Oh, it's not you she's excited to see then, it's the horse treats that she knew were in your pocket?'

He gave her a withering look but she could see humour in his eyes, which was a step forward from the last ten minutes. He ran his hand thoughtfully down the white flash on the horse's nose, which was in direct contrast with the browney-black of the rest of her, apart from some white on the feathering over her ample hooves. He turned to Bridie looking her up and down, taking in the wet ends of her hair under her woolly hat and the wet patches on her coat where the snow had melted and hadn't yet had a chance to dry out. He smiled.

'Come on, let's get you inside so you can follow Mrs H's explicit instructions and get changed out of those clothes and get into the kitchen. I'm fairly sure she'll have a hot meal waiting for you.'

He looked down at Tam, sitting half on his boots.

'You too, let's get you dried off. There's a cushion in front of the fire with your name on it' he laughed as he stroked her. Bridie laughed too because there was *literally* a large cushion with her name on, in its usual place in front of the sitting room fire.

*

Bridie sat on her own, once again.

'I waited for you a while but I wanted to get the washing up done.' said Mrs H.

The concept of a dishwasher was abhorrent to her and the clattering of pans could be heard far and wide as she attacked them with a pan scrubber in the huge butler sink.

'It's fine, it's just good to get some lovely warm food inside me'

She wouldn't admit it, but she was absolutely freezing when she got back and only a long hot shower and a particularly thick roll-neck sweater from Elise's wardrobe had made her thaw out. The dark pink of the sweater clashed horribly with the deep red of her hair, but she was past caring about appearances. She had found some thick woollen leggings which she thought might itch like crazy but didn't.

'That was gorgeous Mrs H. I really needed it' she continued.

She pushed the empty plate away which five minutes before had contained a huge portion of chicken, ham and leek bake with sliced potatoes and lots of veg on the side.

'I can see that - you wolfed it down' Mrs H smiled.

Bridie got up and went to the sink. She could hardly believe it was only 6pm – it felt like bedtime. The sunset had been two hours ago.

After a few moments of drying her plate and mug, Bridie said,

'Mrs H?'

Mrs H looked at her. She knew something very 'Bridie' was coming because she had said her name in that particular way. Mrs Ai-aitch.

'Ye-es' she responded.

'What about decorations? Christmas? decorations?' she asked.

A huge sigh.

'I thought we'd had this conversation before. Ned doesn't celebrate Christmas, therefore - no Christmas decorations.'

'But that's what he does at Christmas. Collect Christmas greenery for Christmas decorations and wreaths!'

Mrs H had to chuckle.

'Yes- ironic isn't it?'

'We could just have a few around the house for tomorrow. I could go out first thing in the morning to collect some holly and stuff.'

'Bridie- leave it, please.'

'If I ask him? If he says no, then I won't push it but he might say yes.'

'Well if it was me I wouldn't mention it but I can't pretend to guess how your mind works, so that's up to you. Just be prepared for him to refuse though. And if there's just going to be the three of us...'

Mrs H looked up at Bridie just in time to catch a thoughtful smile before it changed to an innocent expression. She didn't have time to tell her off before the hallway door opened.

'Bridie, have you finished eating?' Ned didn't wait for an answer but rushed on. 'I wondered if you wanted to come through and have a glass of wine or something warming, in front of the fire?'

Ned looked embarrassed, Bridie looked surprised and Mrs H looked completely flabbergasted. Then she relaxed her expression and smiled as the other two looked at each other awkwardly.

'Go on' she said 'I've got this Christmas cake to finish off for Marcus. No icing but lots of glazed nuts on the top, like a Dundee cake.'

'Don't you need any help?' asked Bridie imploringly, not sure what the summons was for or how much he had heard. He couldn't sack her on Christmas Eve, could he?

'No, I've managed fine by myself all these years' she caught Bridie's expression 'Although I have to say it's been nice having your help and your company this year.' she finished with a smile.

'Would *you* like a glass of anything Mrs H?' asked Ned.

'I'd better not, not yet. I'll have a nice glass of sherry up in my little flat when I go up.'

'If you're sure?' Ned turned to go, catching Bridie's eye.

'I'll be there in a minute' she said as he went through the door.

'What does he want?' she whispered to Mrs H.

'How should I know? I know this though, you're the first member of staff to be invited for a drink in the in the inner sanctum. Although...'

'Although what?'

'Although I'm not sure he thinks of you as a member of staff anymore.' she smiled.

Not catching her meaning, Bridie replied,

'Well, I won't be if he sacks me for insubordination, will I?' and walked nervously down the hallway.

Chapter 18

A Confession

Standing in front of the fireplace with one elbow on top of the mantelpiece, Ned was wearing a low-necked fisherman-style jumper. His dark blonde wavy hair shone in the firelight, his ice blue eyes narrowed and his sensual lips turned up at the edge. Ned only needed a pipe in his hand and a faraway look in his eyes to look like one of those chisel-jawed 60s-style male models from magazine adverts. "Increase your manly attractiveness by buying one of our Seaman Sam sweaters. Only twelve shillings".

He looked positively hunky. The thought was dragged out of Bridie's subconscious reluctantly. She walked over to him and then bent down to stroke the dogs who were lazily wagging their tails at her entrance. They were on their personal cushions, embroidered with Tamsin and Tink.

'I suppose it's so you can tell which one is which?' she asked with a wink.

He laughed out loud despite himself.

'Yes, I usually have trouble telling them apart so the names help' he smiled.

'Do they ever swap cushions just to confuse you?'

Her eyes widened in innocence while his crinkled up in amusement, and then he looked serious.

' Bridie' he started.

'That is a huge log on the fire' she was trying to delay the inevitable. 'It's a huge fire too. It looks more like those fires you get in castles where they used to burn official papers they needed to get rid of and occasionally small body parts that they had hacked off people who displeased them…'

Ned looked aghast.

'Hands, I mean. Hands and fingers. Separately or all together.'

She was rambling now. She was either going to be told off for being too Christmassy or sacked for interfering. The telling off she could deal with, the sacking she couldn't. She really liked this place and its people. She suddenly felt hot and bothered. Fanning her face by grabbing hold of her voluminous neckline and wafting it, she went to sit down on one of the settees.

There were two mid-blue three-seaters placed opposite each other with a low and long polished coffee table in between. The arrangement was meant to promote conversation but Bridie wasn't sure she was ready for it.

'Yes, it does throw out a lot of heat, doesn't it?' he said, taking a seat directly opposite her. 'It's a Yule log.'

She tried to look as if she knew what this meant but he wasn't fooled.

'The Yule log is from one of our trees that had to be cut down. As you probably know, we never cut trees down unless there's a very good reason, say they're either diseased or dying or cut down to make way for a few other trees to grow healthily.'

'I'm glad to hear it. I love trees.'

'The Yule log has to be big as it has to last Twelve nights.'

Derry's words came back to her with a shock.

'Twelve nights?' she asked, wanting to know more. Didn't Twelfth Night end on January 6th - or 5th, she was never sure?

'The Twelfth night always used to end on New Year's Day' he said, 'The original Twelve Nights were from the Midwinter solstice on the 21st of December to the 1st of January, the beginning of the new year. When you think about it, it makes a lot more sense.'

When she did think about it, she realised something else.

'You're still carrying out Christmas traditions even though you don't celebrate Christmas.'

He looked down at his feet.

'Some habits die hard' he said quietly.

'Anyway' he continued into the silence, 'I wanted to talk to you.'

She didn't answer, only nodded.

'I know you're a little confused about the whole Christmas thing.'

He suddenly bent forward and put his head in his hands, then threw his head back to look at her.

'Ah hell, I overheard you and Mrs H in the kitchen last night when I went to take my empty mug back - but then I was trapped. Not daring to move either backwards or forwards.'

Bridie's thoughts raced around, wondering if she'd said anything incriminating. She knew she'd said a lot of things she wouldn't have said if she'd known he was listening.

'I think I need to tell you the whole story' he almost pleaded and this alone was enough to make her just nod silently instead of protesting. He needed to get it off his chest.

'The Christmas morning that my father died, I went to see him early on. The night before had been difficult but as these moods usually passed I hoped that he would be his normal self that day. Although I didn't know what his normal self *was* anymore.

'I took his breakfast tray up as soon as I thought he might be awake. He was sleeping well into the morning some days now and not even bothering to get out of bed. He said he could hardly make it to the bathroom. He had never left his room for two weeks and we were all worried.

'I had made him a present. I thought about it carefully. It took nearly the full two weeks he was confined to his room. I had thought about it for a long time and I hoped it would bring happy memories to the surface. I hoped they would stay there instead of some of the dark images that were playing at the front of his mind now. None of them memories, all of them figments of his fevered imagination.

'Mrs H had made his favourite breakfast just how he liked it. I shouted out to him and pushed the door open. It was never locked in case we needed quick access. His voice came loud and clear.'

'What do *you* want?'

'It was an accusation rather than a question. We had always had a wonderful father-son relationship and this behaviour was killing me even though I knew he couldn't help it. Even though I knew his personality had changed because of the accident. The father I had always known was still there - somewhere underneath the layers - but it was so hard to take.

'I took the tray over to him with a smile on my face and wished him a Merry Christmas. He said, sounding like Scrooge,

'What the hell are you doing boy? Christmas is for people who haven't got anything better to do. Forget all this rubbish!' and he picked my present up and threw it across the floor where it landed beneath the window.

'You' he said pointing his finger at me as though he didn't know me. 'You get back to work. There's always something to be done. Take this foul stuff away with you too. It makes me sick. Get out of here. Go on!' he shouted, his eyes nearly popping out of his head.

I tried to reason with myself that this wasn't my father. This wasn't the brilliant man who brought me and my sister up almost single-handedly after my mother died - but I couldn't. I hated myself for it but I couldn't. I was too upset, angry even. My loving Christmas morning scenario had crumbled into dust.

'I picked up the present lying on the floor and I took it down with the breakfast tray, looking once more at the face of my gentle father, now contorted with rage and went downstairs.'

He stopped now. Bridie found she couldn't speak nor did she want to. She saw his face, distraught now as it would have been eight years ago and she understood everything. He looked at a bag at the far end of the coffee table.

'I need to exorcise my demons' he said gritting his teeth. 'I'm a grown man. I can't go on like this. Listening to you both in the kitchen, I realised that, not only had it affected the way I think about Christmas, it had coloured the way I thought about my father. Both of those need addressing. The second will still be a gradual thing, but perhaps the first…well, we'll see, won't we? Please open it.'

He nodded over at the coarse brown paper bag. Bridie reached for it, put in her hand in pulled out a gaudily wrapped square-shaped Christmas present. She realised what it was.

'Oh God no, I can't. It should be you who opens it.'

'Of course it shouldn't. I know what's in it, don't I? Please unwrap it. Tell me your thoughts.'

She couldn't ignore the entreaty on his face and very slowly began to unwrap the present. It was easy in the end as just two pieces of sellotape held it in place. Probably for ease of opening by his father. She pulled back the paper to reveal a white leather book. No, an album, a photo album. She looked up at Ned for permission and he gave a weak smile as he nodded.

The first page was of a slim smiling, youngish man with a magnificent moustache which curled up at the edges. He looked like he should have been an RAF pilot. In his arms, he held a chubby, smiling baby and the man looked down at him with love shining in his face. A beautiful woman laid her head on his shoulder and held the small fingers of the little blonde baby. Behind them was a magnificent Christmas tree. Bridie looked up at Ned. He looked away towards the fire.

She turned the page to see the same man pushing a girl of about seven and a boy about three, around in a pedal car. They were all laughing and looking up at a figure watching them. She was laughing more than anyone as she surveyed the scene.

The next one taken around the same time, showed the same family all dressed up and grinning from ear to ear. The couple had one arm around each other with the other resting on their children's shoulders.

After this, there were no more photos of the happy laughing lady. A more subdued man, his moustache clipped, still held his children close, a look of love on his face.

A few more pages on and the Christmas tree made another appearance. Everyone was standing in front of it. Mrs H was there, younger and very slightly slimmer but recognisably Mrs H. Henry and Rose stood staring into the camera with slightly self-conscious smiles on their faces, but they were genuine smiles nonetheless.

There were more photos and everyone looked joyful. Every page that Bridie turned showed a happy family and a happy household. They had obviously undergone the tragedy of losing the children's mother, but with the love of everyone around them, they had come through it.

The last photo showed Ned, about ten years younger than he was now, more wide-eyed and innocent, just becoming a man. His father seemed much older, his broad shoulders replaced by a thinner frame - but he was still beaming towards the camera. Father and son with their arms around each other, content in each other's company.

Bridie shut the album quietly and sat for a few minutes staring but not seeing. She was unaware of the tears falling down her cheeks until Ned knelt before her taking her hand.

' Bridie. I'm sorry, I shouldn't have... Are you all right?'

She looked up at him through tear-soaked lashes and then flung her arms around his neck.

'Ned. Oh, Ned.' was all she could say.

Chapter 19

Christmas Eve... Eve!.

The air of peace in the big farmhouse kitchen was remarkable, as it was Christmas Eve. Bridie had imagined it being a hive of activity in preparation for the big day to follow. Of course, she reasoned with herself, the big day wouldn't be much different from any other day in Midwinter Hall. Ned would take his Christmas dinner through on his tray. There could be an addition of a Christmas cracker, but somehow she couldn't see him in a coloured paper hat and chortling at the corny joke from inside it.

Mrs H at least would have her company in this lovely warm kitchen and more to the point, Bridie would have *her* company. No wrapping of presents was happening and no signs of any Christmas decorations to be seen anywhere apart from in their natural habitat in the woods. Ned had vanished again and she wondered if he was keeping out of her sight.

The intense conversation had ended fairly awkwardly. After all, he had bared his soul and she had hugged him tightly as tears ran down their faces. Yet he had said, just before she went out of the room, 'Thank you for listening' and she had replied, 'It was something you needed to say' and they had smiled at each other. She didn't think it would be *too* embarrassing, meeting him again.

'There' said Mrs H, setting a plate of festive flapjacks on the table. 'Will you pour the tea while I check on the Christmas pudding?' There was one thing, when she was finally released from her rather nice hostage situation, she would be a stone heavier. The Christmas pudding was simmering in a huge pan. It would feed an army. Even though Mrs H had a microwave in the kitchen, Bridie had never seen her use it. She liked to do things the old-fashioned way.

Bridie sipped her tea as Mrs H sat back with a sigh.

'Mrs H,' she said and the other woman, recognising the tone, wondered what was coming next. 'Why don't you like being called Yvette? Mrs H isn't even the shorter version as it has three syllables instead of the two in Yvette.'

'It's shorter than the four syllables in Mrs Hooper though' Mrs H smiled. 'Yvette has never suited me. Look at me. I should have a good solid name like Sarah, Mary, Elizabeth, Martha - not Yvette. People expect someone exotic and they get me.'

'I have to say I can see you as a Martha.'

'You see!' Mrs H continued. 'I was named after a film star of my parents' time. My father said that my mother reminded him of her. This Yvette had long blonde hair, elfin features, a slim figure apart from up top and was beautiful.'

'You don't take after your mother then?' asked Bridie and the words were out before she had thought them through. 'Oh! I didn't mean…'

Mrs H was laughing. 'Strangely enough, I do. You see my father was looking at my mother through rose-tinted spectacles because he loved the bones of her.'

Bridie could see the result of a happy family sitting right across the table from her and she smiled back at her happy face.

'Why not just change your name then to Martha or Mary?'

Mrs H took a bite of a cinnamon flapjack and sat back again.

'When I first started here I wasn't long married. The old boss got on well with my husband. We lived in the flat I'm in now. The flat above the stables that Marcus lives in hadn't been converted then - and I like living in the house anyway. No walking across to the Hall in all weathers.'

She nodded over to the window and the snowy scene outside as an example.

'It was Sir Bertie, Ned's father, who first called me Mrs H. There was a popular program at the time, I doubt you'll remember it. The cook was called Mrs H, so Sir Bertie said that they'd got their own Mrs H at the Hall, their own 'treasure' - and he called me by that name ever after.

'Ned did too, as soon as he could talk. His mother, Lady Helga - she was from Norway and it's from her that Ned gets his colouring - always called me Yvette, as she saw Mrs H as derogatory - an insult, but I didn't because it was used with obvious affection. After a while, I became Mrs H and Yvette no longer existed. So yes, I like it, and I'm sorry you have to spend more time saying three syllables instead of two'

Mrs H raised an ironic eyebrow at Bridie who grinned.

'Maybe I could start just calling you H, like a Bond villain.'

'No, you couldn't' said Mrs H.

'It's only one syllable though.'

'No' she pointed a threatening finger at Bridie, her eyebrows lowered but she couldn't stop the corners of her mouth from twitching.

Bridie got up to clear the table.

'I feel that we should be doing something. It's Christmas Eve.'

'Everything is in hand, my love, so stop worrying. All the preparations are done, but if you're wanting to help, you can be in the kitchen at 6:00 a.m. tomorrow. I'll need help then.'

'Ugh' said Bridie but nodded anyway. Mrs H looked over to the fire, her expression dreamy.

'Just the same, you should have seen this kitchen on Christmas Eve in the old days – so busy. Then on Christmas Day, Sir Bertie and Lady Helga with Ned and Elise in the dining room, along with various relatives. All gone now but Ned and Elise. The room was all done out with best tablecloths, candelabra spread down the middle of the table, best dinnerware, crystal glasses…'

She was lost in nostalgia for the old days.

'We all ate in here, in the kitchen. Me, my husband Kenneth and some of the estate workers including Henry and Rose. Ahhh.'

She let out a long sigh and looked around at the quiet kitchen. Neat and tidy and empty apart from herself and Bridie. Bridie could see the sadness in her eyes and changed the subject.

'Where's Ned got to?'

Mrs H came back to the present.

'Oh, out and about. I think he mentioned more logs and coal for Henry and spreading salt and sand on the path so that Henry can get up it on Boxing Day to check his plants in the greenhouse. Ned's forbidden him before then.'

*

Bridie pootled about in the kitchen for a while asking what she could do and when she'd asked it for the tenth, time she realised it was time to get out from under Mrs H's feet.

She thought she'd walk down to the greenhouses where she thought Ned might be with the dogs and offer to take them for a walk. When she got there. Marcus was still shovelling snow that had built up against the glass walls of the greenhouses. He hadn't seen Ned and the dogs for over an hour. No, they weren't at Henry's either as they'd just come from there previously.

She decided to walk around to the stables to see if they were with Bessie, but Bessie wasn't there either. Walking behind the stables to the paddock, there was no sign of the horse there either. Bridie noted with - was that regret? - that the snow seemed thinner on the ground. It was melting very slowly and no more snow had fallen for hours. She looked over at the flower fields, now ploughed and fallow but there was no horse and rider silhouetted there, followed by two dogs. Although Tink would probably ride up at the front of the saddle in state, Queen of all she surveyed.

She stayed out a little longer watching an owl swooping nearby and the dark shape of a hare leaping across this snowy, silent, beautiful landscape. She caught sight of a fox in the distance, its dark form showing against the snow, and felt thrilled. When the snowflakes started falling gently again, she went back inside. Ned would probably be home by now.

The house was quiet though, the dogs conspicuous by their absence. There was no furry greeting for her. She went upstairs to change her trousers which were wet up to her calves. As she pulled out her jeans, she noticed a dress hanging to the right. She had seen it before because it was a beautiful leaf green colour. She pulled it out now and held it against her in front of the mirror. The three-quarter-length sleeves were of chiffon, a shade lighter than the rest of the dress. This chiffon also covered the skirt of the dress which reached to just below mid-calf on her. The bodice was close-fitting and beaded, as was the chiffon skirt, with pale and dark green beads and some extra sparkly ones, that shone like diamonds. It was dazzling.

Could she possibly wear it for Christmas Day then? She realised she would be sitting in the kitchen with Mrs H and regretfully hung it back in the wardrobe. There was a dark green jumper with sparkling sequins that would do for her Christmas Day. Going back downstairs and into the kitchen, Mrs H was energetically scrubbing the wooden table. It would be needed tomorrow before they could use it as their own dining table.

'No Ned? No dogs?' she asked her and before she could answer, there was a noise from the hallway. An unidentifiable swishing noise. Then footsteps accompanied by the scuffling of canine feet and the kitchen door burst open.

'Mrs H, how many people will your Christmas dinner feed?' shouted Ned, brandishing a large torch.

Mrs H. looked taken aback.

'Well, let's see. You, me, Bridie - and I cook one for Marcus. Henry and Rose usually cook their own but not this year because of the fuel and I've accounted for them so…'

'So you could feed seven easily?' Ned asked. Bridie answered.

'From what I've seen, she could feed the population of a small village.' Ned relaxed and smiled.

'Good, good' he muttered, then asked again more loudly 'Here in the Hall?'

Mrs H and Bridie faced each other with identical expressions of wide-eyed and open-mouthed amazement.

'Yes' spluttered Mrs H.

'Splendid' he said and then turned to Bridie. 'And can you do something with these?' She followed him into the hallway and there, laid in abundance on one of the tarpaulins on the floor, were branches of fir with pine cones attached, strings of dark green ivy, branches of holly, their bright red berries sparkling as they reflected the lamplight - and bunches of mistletoe.

Bridie stared down at it and then at the expectant look on Ned's face. She found she couldn't get the words out but the wide, happy smile on her face was all that Ned needed.

Chapter 20

Late Christmas Eve.

'Where are we going to hang the mistletoe?' Bridie laughed, holding a large bunch above her head. To her surprise, Ned didn't laugh but coloured up and turned his back on her and said in a strangulated voice to just 'weave it amongst the boughs, that's what we used to do'.

He obviously didn't see it as the joke it was meant to be, thought Bridie, who was beginning to feel like a floozy now. It was only a joke, wasn't it? The fact that it might have been based on wishful thinking made *her* cheeks blush now too.

She took the mistletoe into the sitting room and practised weaving on the two fir branches on top of the huge mantelpiece. Yes, it looked good. She took another look at the pine cones peeping from all over the boughs. She had suggested spray painting them gold and asked if he had any gold paint anywhere. He said it wasn't something he routinely shopped for and besides they look much better in their natural form, like most things did.

She had thought 'killjoy' but now she could see what he meant. It was starting to look like the illustrations in Christmas magazines. In fact, it was starting to look a lot like Christmas, as they say. He was right, damn him.

In the hallway, Ned was draping greenery from the chandelier while standing on a stepladder. Bridie grabbed some of the ivy and started winding it through the spindles of the central staircase. After adding holly and fir, it was looking good but it was missing something. She stood back and realised what it was.

'Christmas lights, fairy lights, have you got any?' He looked taken aback and thought for a moment.

'We did have many years ago. I have no idea where they are now or whether I got rid of them. We don't need them anyway.'

'Christmas tree?' she attempted.

'I'll just nip into town through the treacherous conditions and see if I can pick one up from a shop that has stayed open late on Christmas Eve, especially for us, shall I?'

'Real Christmas tree?' she attempted again.

'I'm not cutting down a healthy tree just to make you happy.'

'You cut down perfectly healthy flowers to sell for your business.'

'Which would have died off anyway if left and I use their seeds to sow again.'

'Okay' she said, as unusually she didn't have anything else to add.

They carried on decorating until the sitting room, the hallway, the kitchen and the porch in front of the house were decked with greenery with bright red berries and natural un-gilded pine cones. Bridie persuaded him to do the dining room too in case they used that. He was adamant that they would all eat in the kitchen where it was warmer but added a few branches here and there. Bridie sneaked in afterwards and added more greenery.

It was all gone now. Ned took the tarpaulin outside and shook it. As soon as Tam and Tink heard the door open they flew through the kitchen door, which banged against the wood panelling making Ned flinch. He looked down at them sitting next to him in the snow, expectantly.

'Come on then, we'll walk round to the stables to say good night to Bessie.'

As if they understood him, they trotted ahead of him, around the back of the house in the direction of the stables. Bridie had always loved how he talked to them as though they understood his every word. Now she was beginning to believe that they did.

'Can I come with you?' she asked as he came in to grab his coat and thick boots.

'Of course' he smiled. She felt quite included in the Midwinter family now as he said that and quickly pulling her own boots and coat on, she skipped after him, nearly as giddy as the two dogs.

She watched Tink do a dance which involved all four legs going in different directions. She started laughing until she too stepped on the icy patch and had to be rescued by Ned, holding his hands out to her. She felt the same electric shock feeling she had experienced before, especially when she gained firm footing and her face was inches away from his. She realised that she was still holding his hands and it felt good. He looked like he felt the same and his face came even closer to hers and he lifted one hand up to stroke her face. She could feel his breath on her lips and she started to close her eyes.

The next minute, despite Ned's tight grip on her hand, she danced again like Bambi on the ice and then ended up doing the splits. He pulled her up once more. Ned recovered first.

'Are you all right? That looked painful.'

She glared at him as she realised he was laughing. Even Tink was giving her a 'now you know what it feels like' look.

'I'm fine, thank you' she said, her nose in the air.

She let go of his hand which was actually the last thing she wanted to do and marched off in the direction of the stables. Things ended okay though on the way back as Ned hooked her arm through his in case of further acrobatics and they looked at each other and laughed. When they reached the porch they kicked the snow off their boots and went inside.

''I suppose' he began awkwardly 'that I ought to have an early night. Busy day tomorrow.'

'For all of us.' agreed Bridie,

'I'll erm, leave you then.'

Bridie loved the look of regret in his eyes. The fact that he was so unsure of saying anything else. Perhaps there was nothing else to say, but things seem to have changed between them. There were indications earlier but tonight...

'I'll, well, I'll see you in the morning then.'

He leant forward and kissed her cheek - but the way he squeezed her upper arms spoke volumes.

'Bright and early' she replied with a happy smile, giving him an extra peck on the cheek, just because she felt like she could.

*

As soon as Ned had gone up the stairs, Bridie raced through to the kitchen expecting to find Mrs H there. She was shocked to see a darkened kitchen and when she switched the lights on it was obvious that everything was turned off and Mrs H had retired to bed. She looked at the clock. 10:50 p.m. She didn't know why she expected that Mrs H would be chained to the kitchen eternally but she did.

Of course Mrs H would have had an early night. If anyone needed her sleep so she could be up early, it was her. Bridie made a mental note that she would do anything she could to help her in the morning. Unfortunately, she didn't make a mental note not to disturb Mrs H tonight because she made her way across to the door in the corner of the kitchen. Opening the door, she went up the winding stairs. She wondered how much longer Mrs H could manage these stairs and then realised that these stairs had probably kept her as fit as she was. Besides, she loved her little flat and she would never move out of it. Ned would probably install a chair lift for her, knowing him.

She gave a tentative knock at the door at the top.

'Come in' came Mrs H's voice. Too trusting by far, it could have been a deranged psychotic Santa, wanting to kidnap her to work in the toy mines in Lapland for eternity. Reining in her imagination, she entered and found a lovely cosy room lit with yellow glowing lamps and smelling separately of cinnamon and a scent of jasmine.

'What are you doing here at this time?' she said, indicating the chair at the other side of the fire. Bridie sat down.

' I'm sorry to disturb you, but I wondered if you knew where the Christmas decorations were that were used when Sir Bertie was alive. Specifically, any lights?'

'Lights? Look, sit down and have a sherry with me while I have a think.'

She stood up and went across to a mahogany cabinet which pulled down to reveal various bottles of alcohol, which had probably been there since her husband's day. Bridie wasn't a fan of sherry anyway, thinking of the dark, sickly sweet concoction she was offered at her godmother's. However, this was quite pleasant and light. She had another sip.

'I have to say' said Mrs H, settling back into her fireside chair, 'that I think Ned threw all the decorations away.' She looked apologetic as Bridie grimaced. 'If there are any left they'll be up in the attic.'

Bridie had a feeling that they would be. She hadn't noticed any when they were up there on their 'top field' search but there *were* lots of boxes and it was the only chance she had.

'Do you think it would be all right for me to have a look?'

'Isn't it a bit late tonight?' said Mrs H and then noticing Bridie's look of disappointment added, 'but I suppose there's no harm in having a quick look.'

Bridie smiled and was in no rush to finish the unexpectedly nice sherry. It was very homely up here and she could understand why Mrs H loved it so much. As she went, she looked out of the window onto a wonderful snowy vista.

'No sign of Santa yet' she said 'I hope you've been good.'

She turned towards Mrs H who replied.

'Don't you worry about me, but I'm wondering if *you're* on the naughty list.'

They both laughed and hugged each other, wishing each other a Merry Christmas. Then Bridie went along the landing towards the attic door.

Chapter 21

Christmas Morning - Let There Be Light

'What on…?'

Ned could be heard through the open kitchen door. Bridie smiled at Mrs H but received a furrowing of the brow in exchange.

'Too much, too soon?' she asked.

'We'll soon find out' Mrs H replied as Ned came through into the kitchen.

'Lights? Artificial ones? After what I said last night?' he asked.

He wasn't angry, more confused. Perhaps he wasn't used to having his word taken so lightly.

'I know, but I thought if you just saw them' she appealed.

He shook his head in frustration but turned towards the garland draped down through the spindles of the staircase. It now twinkled merrily due to the lights threaded through it. He stood and looked at it for a moment, then walked down the hall into the sitting room. His eyes searched the room finding the twinkly bits across the great mantle within the garlands that topped it. He turned to her as she loitered in the doorway.

'Where else?' he asked.

'Everywhere there is Christmas greenery' she replied, opening her arms wide as if it was a silly question.

'Of course' he said.

'The lights look good don't they?' she asked, wanting his approval.

He looked at the staircase again and his eyes crinkled up. He cleared his throat.

'They look all right I suppose, but it's 6:15 in the morning. Isn't it a little early for Blackpool Illuminations?'

'It's never too early for fairy lights and it's hardly Blackpool Illuminations. You didn't have many so I've had to be very frugal with them.'

'What are you doing up at this time anyway?'

' I promised Mrs H that I'd help her this morning. She's actually been up since 5:00 a.m.

She's already baked these delicious little cakes for breakfast which–'

'Yule cakes!' he grinned and charged past her into the kitchen. Mrs H already had the warm Yule cakes on the plate, so they sat down at the table and reached for the butter. Ned cut a slice of cheese too, but Bridie wasn't sure how she felt about that. They weren't really cakes, more like puffier, lighter Hot Cross buns with candied peel and cinnamon. Not a word was said until they had finished every crumb and Ned had reached for another, then Mrs H interrupted the silence.

'Merry Christmas Ned' she smiled.

'Oh yes, Merry Christmas to you Mrs H and to you too, Bridie.'

Bridie wished him Merry Christmas. 'I would have said it to you earlier but you were too busy telling me off.'

'I wasn't telling you off' he protested 'Not exactly.'

He finished off and was standing up to go and check the greenhouse. Mrs H stopped him before he could get out of the kitchen.

'Seven?' she said.

He frowned at her in bewilderment.

'You asked if I could do dinner for seven. Well, there's only six of us.'

Bridie mentally counted up. She was right.

'Yes, I counted Zinnia' he said.

This produced the reaction he obviously didn't want as he looked embarrassed. When Bridie said,

'That's brilliant. I'm so glad she's coming.' He shuffled his feet a little.

'That's just it. I went all the way up to her house taking Bessie, as I know she's a favourite of hers and she said no.'

'No?' echoed Bridie, finding it hard to believe that Zinnia had turned down the offer of an olive branch.

'She wasn't offensive. She just felt that she wouldn't fit in here and she would rather spend it by herself. I tried to persuade her but, in the end, it's her decision. I've called this morning but she's not answering the phone.'

'That's such a shame' said Bridie sadly with Mrs H nodding in agreement.

'Bessie? You took Bessie through the Silent Wood?'

He let out a bark of a laugh.

'I tried but she just stood at the edge looking up through the trees as usual, so I ended up walking the rest of the way after I tied her to one of the oak branches'

He started to leave again but after moving each dog from the front of the Aga for the twentieth time, Mrs H said,

'And take these two with you, out from under my feet.'

He laughed and called them both. They came over very slowly, but whether it was the warmth they didn't want to leave or all the food surrounding them. Bridie wasn't quite sure

*

As cooking and baking weren't Bridie's strengths, she set herself on doing the menial tasks. Washing up, checking on pans and ovens, basting the huge turkey. Although after the last basting when she had nearly tipped hot fat on herself, she was sent to do something out of harm's way.

'Go and fetch the best cutlery from the dining room dresser. You can give it a quick polish. You won't be able to set it out until I've finished on this table.'

The kitchen table now looked like a scene of chaos with every inch of it taken up by food or cooking utensils. As it was Mrs H, it was somehow an *orderly* chaos.

'When you've done that you can bring the best plates through and give them a wipe too.'

Bridie started down the hall thoughtfully. Such a shame to have to cart it all through there. Then she would have to wait until she could lay the table until the very last minute. She took a peek at what was in the dresser, its drawers and its cupboards - and then went back through.

'I'm laying the table properly in the dining room so you don't have to rush to clear this table.'

'Oh no you don't.'

She waved a wooden spoon at Bridie and a blob of cream dropped off and fell on the kitchen floor with no dog there to lick it up.

'You said 'too much too soon' earlier about the lights and that worked out, didn't it?'

'The last time the formal dining room was used for Christmas was the year before Ned's father died. Ned only uses it for business meetings now, entertaining clients and suppliers.'

'What a waste then. Instead of having dull dinners…'

Mrs H coughed.

'…Instead of having wonderful dinners served to dull people and the room drowning in business speak, it could be reverberating to the sound of laughter and merriment, the smells of

Christmas food, music to delight the ears, smiles and happiness all around....'

'Have you been watching too many soppy Christmas films?' asked Mrs H. incredulously.

'All right, that might be a bit over the top' said Bridie as she stopped jumping about and waving her hands in the air. 'But you get my meaning.'

'Yes, I do' admitted Mrs H 'but on your own head be it.'

'I take full responsibility' said Bridie, trying and failing to execute the Brownie sign of honour. Mrs H laughed and then her eyes went slightly out of focus. She was many years in the past.

'Although it would be nice to see it how it used to be' she whispered and caught sight of the lights shimmering and glowing in the greenery above the fireplace in the kitchen. 'and the lights look lovely.'

Bridie was pleased.

'If you like those lights, just wait until you see–' she stopped.

'Bridie!' Mrs H. warned in *that* voice.

'Like I said, just you wait and see' and, grabbing some tea towels, she went quietly through into the dining room.

*

Just over an hour later, Bridie shut the dining room door and leaned back against it, feeling pleased with herself. She toyed with the idea of bringing Mrs H to see it, but she wanted it to be a surprise for her too. Instead, she popped into the kitchen and shouted across. 'Do you need me for just now? I'm just going out to do something.'

Mrs H popped her head around the side of an open cupboard door.

'Not just now, so you can get up to whatever mischief you want.'

'Mrs H!' gasped Bridie, 'Mischief? Me?'

'Let's just say I've got your measure, young lady.' she laughed ' but be back here in an hour or so as it will be all hands on deck. Although Ned's bringing Henry and Rose up soon and I know Rose will want to help.'

' Not too many cooks?' asked Bridie.

'Not with Rose. We work well together. She always helped out at Christmas gatherings' said Mrs H and stuck her head back inside the cupboard to resume her search.

Bridie pulled on her outdoor clothing and went to look for Marcus, who she hoped wasn't in the same place as Ned. She eventually found him outside Bessie's stable.

'There you are. Are you ready? Is Ned around?'

Marcus gave her a composed look.

'Luckily for you, he's in the end greenhouse mending one of the heaters before it gets any worse. Then he's going down to Henry and Roses to have a quick sherry before he brings them up to the Hall. So I should have time to do what you wanted.'

'I've left the box around the corner of the study door covered by a blanket. Don't tell Mrs H, I'll say I did it, Marcus. I promise' She looked worried. 'I don't want to get you into trouble.'

'I know you don't. I don't mind. He'll know it was your idea anyway.'

Another one who's got my character pinned down, thought Bridie. She looked into the stable.

'Why is Bessie saddled up?'

'Ned was going to ride her around the field for a bit of exercise but he's had to do this repair job, so I'm taking it off her.'

'Don't' said Bridie suddenly as a thought came to her in a series of words as usual – Zinnia. Bessie. Favourite. Wood. Dinner, until they formed an idea.

'I'll take her for a bit of exercise myself around the woodland path and back again. Don't worry. I won't go and gallop her full pelt across snowy fields.'

'And you say you don't want to get me into trouble? Can you even ride?' he asked quite reasonably. After all, this *was* Bridie. She looked affronted in a jokey way.

'Marcus Wendell, I have ridden the finest Arab stallions through the High Atlas mountains of Morocco!'

Which was unlikely for a librarian, she had to admit but thanks to her unconventional parents, it was completely true. She had been a natural on a horse but hadn't ridden for a few years now. It was like riding a bike though, it wasn't something you forgot.

' Really?' he said, not sure if she was joking or not.

'Yes, I promise you I am very proficient at horse riding.' She looked at him seriously and his face cleared of worry.

'All right but on your own head be it.'

She'd heard that exact phrase from Mrs H's lips earlier. Soon she'd be balancing so much on her head that she'd start to sink into the ground, singing 'All the Good Girls Go to Hell' by Billie Eilish.

Five minutes later with Marcus already on with his task, Bridie let Bessie out whilst talking to her, hoisted herself into the saddle, tickled between the old horse's ears and set off in the direction of the Silent Wood.

Chapter 22

Christmas Day

As she rode Bessie slowly up to the woodland track, she wondered if Zinnia would still be able to ride a horse, as fond as she was of Bessie. Then she remembered Marcus laughing when she talked about Zinnia being an old lady, a few weeks ago. She's probably fitter than you are, he'd declared.

How old was she? Difficult to say. Bridie knew she was retired and her husband had been quite a bit older than her. She didn't seem old. She was almost ageless. Although she appeared to be stuck in the time of her youth as a perennial hippie, a bit like Bridie's parents. Thinking about it, the actual hippie era had taken place possibly when Zinnia was too young and well before her own parents' time. Perhaps Emlyn, Zinnia's husband had been the true hippie and she had become absorbed into the creed, which wasn't a bad one as far as Bridie could see. If you took away the drug abuse, cults, naked cavorting at festivals and feather brains because of the mind-altering drugs... she stopped in her thoughts. That part of hippies was pretty damning. Yet there was love, peace and Nature in the movement and all these could be enjoyed without the other things that dragged the hippie movement down. Love, Peace and Nature was good.

She had nearly reached the pathway into the silent wood. She made Bessie face square onto the path and pressed gently on her sides, clicking with her tongue for encouragement. No, it was no good. Bessie had planted her hooves squarely on the ground and wouldn't budge.

Bridie dismounted and, stroking Bessie's muzzle, tied her to a strong oak branch. As she prepared to walk like Ned had, to persuade Zinnia, Bessie gave a low-pitched nicker and put her head up, her ears on high alert. Looking down the path, a feeling of excitement started in Bridie's stomach. She could see that same glow she had seen before. Green, yellow, indescribable really.

Gently, she took hold of Bessie's bridle and pulled very slightly. Nothing - but after a moment Bessie quietly put one hoof forward, then another. Very carefully, Bridie led the old horse down the path into the Silent Wood where it was thought that all animals feared to tread. Bessie kept her head up and her eyes on the old oak glowing on the left side of the path. Bridie noted that it was on the opposite side of the path to where she had first seen Derry.

Slowly, reverently, silently, they went on until they reached the giant oak. Bessie stopped of her own accord. She turned to face the oak which was now sending out gentle rays of translucent light in their direction. Suddenly the light became stronger and began to pulsate. There was a movement from Bessie, pulling the bridle out of her hand, so Bridie was left as a mere observer.

Her body ran hot and cold as she watched this old workhorse bow her head towards the tree in reverence, one foreleg straight and the other bent in an equine imitation of a courtly bow. Bridie's breath caught in her throat. She stopped all movement as though she were in suspended animation. Then as she slowly looked up at the tree, she saw Derry half emerge from within its trunk. Derry reached a half-transparent arm out towards Bessie. Her outstretched hand, palm down, hovered an inch above Bessie's forelock but the light continued down, lighting the whole head.

Nothing was said and this time, Derry didn't acknowledge Bridie's existence at all, instead concentrating on Bessie. It was almost like two old friends greeting each other. The ease of recognition was there.

Just as Derry withdrew her hand, she turned her face towards Bridie and smiled. She saw that Derry had aged, perhaps twenty years. She was still so incredibly beautiful though and Bridie was still smiling back as she disappeared back into the oak tree completely. She took a deep but shaky breath, thought for a moment then turned to face Bessie. At the same moment. Bessie turned to her and they faced one another, their thoughts attuned. Bessie eased her muzzle gently forward to Bridie's face and Bridie put her lips against the soft skin as she put her arms around Bessie's neck. She realised with surprise that tears were falling down her cheeks. Bessie seemed to acknowledge this with a soft nicker before Bridie pulled herself together.

'Come on my lovely girl' she said 'we're going to fetch Zinnia.

*

Leading Bessie gently on the rein, they both walked quietly up the woodland path. The daylight soon appeared at the end highlighting the snow as in a snowscape vista, viewed between two large trees, their boughs bending over to form an arch.

Bridie reached the opening first and looked up across the top field. To her surprise, Zinnia was already halfway down it. She looked up, surprised to see Bridie. As Bessie caught up and stood next to Bridie, Zinnia's jaw dropped and she came to a sudden halt. She then quickened her step, making towards the wood and was soon standing in front of them.

'How on earth?' she began, looking at Bessie and going over to make a fuss of her.

'I was surprised too but she wanted to come in. I didn't make her.'

'Ned told me he couldn't make her move into the wood for love nor money yesterday.'

'She was hesitant until she saw… until she saw the glow inside the tree.'

'Glow.' Zinnia said this word in an awed whisper. She knows, thought Bridie.

'Yes, she walked over to it, bowed down, then we continued on.'

'Bowed!' Zinnia's eyes were as round as saucers.

'That's what it seemed like.'

There was a pause.

'Did you see anything else?'

'Anything else? Like what? What should I have seen?'

Bridie wanted to make the woman talk but she was having none of it.

'It doesn't matter' she said, head down, staring at the ground in front of her.

'Anyway' Bridie clapped her hands making Bessie give her a sideways look. 'I was coming to fetch you to let you ride on Bessie but I'm pleased to see you were coming to Midwinter Hall anyway.'

Zinnia cleared her throat and looked away.

'Actually, I was just coming down to the wood to find a little peace on Christmas Day.'

'So you weren't coming to the Hall?'

'No, I was–'

'Looking for 'anything else'?'

'Perhaps.' Zinnia stuck out her chin defiantly. 'but if you must know, this wood is where I feel closest to Emlyn. It was our spiritual place. I feel his presence more here than I do at the house.'

'I'm sorry' Bridie said feeling genuinely sad for her. 'I would leave you alone - but I really want you to come back to the Hall with us and Ned does too - and everyone.'

'It's very nice of you to go to this trouble, but what with all this going on over the donkeys and the field, I think the atmosphere will not be conducive to a good Christmas.' She frowned. 'It's funny. I thought Ned didn't celebrate Christmas ever since his father died?'

'Which makes it even more important that you *are* there. It's the first time since then that the whole household will be eating together. It's very special. You need to be there.'

'Oh, I didn't realise that.' Zinnia seemed on the verge of agreeing to come to the Hall, 'but this ongoing problem between me and Ned regarding the field and the passage through the sacred wood, it's unsurmountable.'

Bridie put her hands on her hips.

'Of course it isn't. No problem is so bad that a solution can't be found, especially one as, let's face it, trivial as this.'

'It's not trivial though - not to me.'

' I understand about the sanctity of the wood, but you're blocking your mind off. There will be a way and it's not going to take a team of rocket scientists to come up with it either. Think about it, woman!'

Zinnia looked taken aback and a little scared of this new Bridie.

'And while we're at it, Ned in his new tentative approach to Christmas has laid all his doubts aside about the dispute on rehoming those poor old donkeys and has come to you, holding an olive branch. He swallowed his pride and asked you to the first proper Christmas he's had in what, eight or nine years? And you say no. You're both as bad as each other with your stubbornness but I have to say that you, Zinnia, take the crown. Doesn't it seem almost self-pitying that you would rather spend the day by yourself with no fuel and possibly no proper Christmas dinner, when you could just accept the hand of friendship that is being offered to you?'

There was an uncomfortable silence.

'I have to say' said Zinnia eventually, 'that you are the most opinionated girl I have met. You say exactly what you think without worrying if you will offend anyone.'

Bridie thought about this for a moment. 'That's right. In a nutshell. I usually just call it the uncomfortable truth.' she offered.

Zinnia's face split into a grin.

'I may not have been so ready to forgive if I didn't think you were completely right in everything you said'

Bridie, through the mask of bravado she had been wearing, let out a sigh of relief. She wasn't really that hard – but sometimes, things just needed to be said.

'Does that mean you'll come with us, back to the Hall?'

'If you think Ned will still want me there?'

'He will. Come on, let's go to Midwinter.'

And so it was that twenty minutes later, a surprised Ned saw Bridie leading a beaming Zinnia down towards the hall on the very sprightly-looking Bessie. Zinnia dismounted and as Marcus came up to take Bessie, the two smiled at each other before Zinnia went up to Ned.

'I hope you can forgive me. I've been pig-headed' she said.

'We both have' he smiled. 'Welcome to Midwinter Hall - and Merry Christmas.'

Chapter 23

Christmas Dinner

There was no awkwardness as Bridie had at first feared. Everyone hugged each other. Zinnia had obviously been well-liked before and the little problem hadn't changed that. Tam and Tink greeted everyone, wanting to join in. Everyone made a fuss of them. Tink's ears were permanently pricked up in delight and Tam's enthusiastic tail wagging was creating a draught.

Ned offered everyone a drink but despite trying to treat them all as guests, everyone, including Ned, was soon at work in the kitchen or doing some practical tasks in the house.

There was more wood and coal to be brought in, and more fires to be built up. There was washing up, drying up and checking. Bridie was sure that Mrs H could have managed it all single-handedly - well perhaps with Rose's help

- but she seemed like she was enjoying the camaraderie.

Bridie slipped away for a while and came back into the kitchen later without anyone noticing as they were so intent on their tasks.

'You can all relax for now, your starters will be on the table in twenty minutes' said Mrs H.

'Mrs H' asked Ned after this announcement. 'Do you want this table cleared so we can lay it for dinner?'

Mrs H looked guiltily at Bridie and kept quiet. Ned turned to Bridie with a questioning look. Bridie hardly missed a beat.

'Does it look like we can clear this table so we can all sit down?' she asked.

From Ned's hopeless expression, the answer was no. Bridie took a deep breath.

'Would you all like to follow me?'

Ned frowned, Mrs H looked worried but everyone else was content to follow Bridie, not to say a little intrigued. She headed in the direction of the dining room. She turned to Marcus who nodded and she nodded back.

'Mrs H, you too' she called.

Mrs H raised her eyes to heaven but knew she couldn't get out of it and bustled through to join the others. They stood outside the dining room.

'Not the dining room?' Ned was incredulous. 'You're taking too much on yourself. Why have you done this? I don't use this room now, you should know that. I did say we were dining in the kitchen where it's warm and welcoming and…'

'…completely cluttered. There are seven of us. Ned - we need to leave Mrs H in peace.'

Bridie stared Ned down.

'All right. I agree but it probably feels damp in here and cold.'

Bridie ignored him and reached out to open the door. Standing to one side, she watched their faces as they passed her. First was Ned who stopped dead at the sight. Zinnia had to prod his back to make him move so everyone else could get in. One by one they entered, each of them silent, taking in the sight and turning round slowly except for Mrs H who was the last one in. She took one look at the room. It was just how she described it to Bridie, only better. Tears came to her eyes as she tried to comprehend what she saw.

Pine branches, pine cones, holly and ivy with sprigs of rosemary and bay were laid across the mantlepiece and the windowsills. Fairy lights glittered in each display. At the far side of the fireplace stood an old, small, Christmas tree, artificial and obviously very well loved. Bridie had been worried about this after finding it in the attic but felt it had a place here this Christmas. From its freshly cleaned, dark green branches hung her gingerbread men, iced with elf hats and Santa hats and even a couple with antlers.

On the long oak table was a fresh, brilliant white tablecloth. Placemats of green and red denoted where each of the seven would sit. Candles in single holders stretched down the table with a candelabra in the middle, throwing a refracting light on the crystal glasses, which were waiting there to be filled.

Three high candles were spaced along the mantle above the greenery and cast their light in the over-mirror, throwing a gentle glow around the room. There was one tall candle in each of the two windows, nestling into the fir branch and the flames reached up, reflecting in the window. A double flame.

The best crockery and cutlery shone on the table making the most of its unaccustomed outing. In the old stone fireplace with its ornate iron grate, a leaping fire, set by Marcus, warmed the whole room, its red and yellow flames reaching out to every corner, to heat and caress.

As they watched, one of the logs dropped, sending a myriad of sparks up the chimney.

This noise seemed to break the spell. No one had uttered a word as they looked around in wonder. Now they all looked at Ned expectantly. He was still taking it all in steadily but his expression was that of a child, thrilling to the magic of Christmas. He seemed to come to and looked across at Bridie who stood there, expectantly.

'Have you done this Bridie?' he asked. She didn't know whether to claim responsibility or not but her promise to Mrs. H came back to bite her on the bum.

'Yes, it's all my idea'. she said reluctantly.

He stepped towards her and put his hands on her shoulders.

'It's wonderful' he whispered pulling her towards him and kissing her on the cheek.

Bridie seemed to hear a very audible sigh of relief from Mrs H. as everyone gathered around her, saying how beautiful it looked. Zinnia was counting the place settings. There were seven - so Bridie had been confident she would get Zinnia to come down today. The older woman smiled to herself.

'It's set for seven' said Henry as if reading Zinnia's mind. 'Are you sure you don't mind us eating in here with you?' It was hard to rid himself of the servant/master mentality that had existed when he was younger. Ned pulled him in for a hug, which predictably both pleased and embarrassed Henry.

'I can't think of anything I'd like more' he said.

*

Fortified by a mildly alcoholic apple and orange punch, everyone had 'mucked in' and the starters had been put on the table. Tam and Tink were more than happy to sprawl on their beds in the warmth of the kitchen. They had both already had their special Christmas lunch and were full, content and sleepy.

Henry, Rose, Marcus and Mrs H placed themselves furthest away from Ned and it was left to Zinnia and Bridie to take the places next to him at the head of the table. Just before the starters commenced, Ned went out, whispering to Mrs H who fished some champagne flutes out of the sideboard to go with the bottle of champagne that Ned returned with.

'I would just like to toast you all for making Christmas come alive for me again' he said, pouring a toast into the glasses, with Henry and Rose insisting on just enough for a small mouthful. He passed the glasses out and went on.

'I would like to thank Mrs H for the magnificent feast she has prepared for us - and I want to thank Bridie here, for cajoling, bullying and being as secretive as MI5, to make sure I started to enjoy Christmas once more.'

Everyone laughed as Bridie said 'Bullying?' in an aggrieved fashion.

'To Mrs H, to Bridie and to all of you' he said, raising his glass. After a sip, Bridie held her own glass up.

'And to Ned- and to Midwinter Hall - and to many more Christmases to come.'

They all held their glasses up for the toast before finishing off the contents.

'I'd better get more champagne' Ned stated.

'No, you don't' said Mrs H, 'sit down and get your starter. There's white wine on the table and I don't want you taking the edge of your appetites.'

'Have you two got your homemade wine for later?' he added expectantly.

Mrs H and Rose nodded with a smile.

'Oh dear' replied Ned.

Bridie looked puzzled, while Mrs H caught her eye and laughed but didn't elaborate, apart from to say 'I don't think they're *that* alcoholic, young man.'

The salmon and avocado terrine was delicious. Served up with small, warm, homemade bread buns. There was still a slight awkwardness from Zinnia and because of her reticence to join in, the starters were mostly eaten in an amicable silence. The first course settled and the second bottle of white wine being half empty, tongues had loosened and Zinnia had responded to Ned's query by describing her childhood Christmases in Devon.

She had moved to a commune in Wales when she was only twenty and that's when she met Emlyn. Their Christmas meal in the commune consisted mostly of beans and cabbages that they'd grown- and lots and lots of homemade alcohol.

At this, Mrs H and Rose looked at each other and smiled before Mrs H glanced at the clock and hurried out, with Rose hard on her heels. After a minute or two, Bridie followed them and they all reappeared carrying various dishes piled high with food. The menfolk made their way into the kitchen to fetch more, while Zinnia arranged everything on the table. When everyone was seated Ned stood up.

'For what Nature has provided us with, we are truly thankful.'

They all clicked their glasses together and shouted 'Wassail'

Bridie looked puzzled at the departure from the traditional grace- and from the usual 'cheers'. Ned whispered to her as he clinked glasses with her. 'It means 'Be of good health'

She looked down the table and felt the thrill of everything coming together. In the middle, in pride of place was a large cooked turkey with a golden skin. There were slices cut off and laid on the platter for everyone to help themselves. In front of Ned was a large honey-glazed ham which he set about carving. Dotted around the table were buttered Brussels sprouts with bacon, red cabbage, light but crispy roast potatoes, glistening glazed carrots, a steaming bowl of peas and butter and roast caramelized parsnips. There was also mashed swede with black pepper and gravy boats of proper gravy dotted around. Lastly, there was a huge dish of light and fluffy…

' …Yorkshire puddings?' exclaimed Zinnia in surprise and looked at Bridie who having heard all about this from Mrs H just grinned back.

'Ah' Ned smiled, 'coming from the Christmas dinners of Devon and Wales, you'll realise you haven't lived until you've had Yorkshire puddings with Christmas dinner.'

Chapter 24

A Musical Interlude

Everyone managed a little of Mrs H's excellent Christmas pudding with brandy butter before they collapsed against the back of the chairs. Henry spoke for all of them when he said he was 'full to busting!' Ned led them through to the sitting room for a coffee as Mrs H and Rose cleared the table. Zinnia looked around at the natural decorations there with pleasure and her eyes alighted on the large fireplace.

'Is that a yule log?' she beamed.

'It is' replied Ned. 'It's been burning steadily since the solstice and with a bit of good management should last the Twelve Nights of Yule.'

Ned went across to the windows to draw the curtains.

'No!" Bridie shouted louder than she meant to. Ned looked at her in surprise. 'It's just that it's nice being cosy in here when we can see the dark snowy landscape out there' she tried.

'I would have thought it would be cosier still with the curtains drawn?' countered Ned.

She fixed Ned with a zen-like stare and eventually with a sigh, Ned let go of the curtains.

Bridie waited until the coffee was served and everyone was sitting down, then sharing a quick glance with Marcus, she went out into the hallway and into the porch, where she bent down to two black boxes, one on each side. When she came back, Mrs H, who was sitting facing towards the window, had her mouth open wide.

'What *have* you been up to Bridie?'

At this, everyone turned to look through the windows. There, casting a soft glow onto the snow beneath it, one of the White Pines sparkled with old-fashioned lantern lights, making the pine needles glisten. The moon was out, adding its own silvery light to the Christmassy scene - with the stars adding some festive twinkles of their own to the occasion.

There were lots of excited exclamations and everyone sounded thrilled apart from Ned, who stood with his nose pressed against one of the window panes without saying a word. Bridie moved to stand next to him as everyone went back to their coffees. He still didn't say anything and his expression was unreadable. Slowly he turned to look at her, swallowed hard, then turned to look at the tree once more- but this time, he put his arm around Bridie's shoulders drawing her into his body.

Bridie snuggled in happily. She couldn't help it. She had fought this feeling probably from the first day she met him but the thrill she felt when she was near him spoke volumes. She was falling in love with this man.

From behind this scene, as the others chatted, Mrs H and Rose watched the two figures at the window and smiled happily across at each other.

*

After coffee, Bridie asked if she could fetch a book from the study.

'Of course you can, you don't have to ask' was the answer, which pleased Bridie no end.

She came back with the small book she had found before – Christmas Customs Through the Ages.

'Ah, my great-grandmother's book' Ned exclaimed.

'I thought it might have been your father's?' said Bridie.

'It was- I meant my great-grandmother wrote it.'

'But it says, G.M.Chichester' said Bridie in surprise.

'She used her maiden name, Gertrude Mary Chichester. The reason being that her husband, my great-grandfather was the author of a few books on folklore and she didn't want to ride on his coat tails.'

'Wow' said Bridie with feeling. What an interesting family she had come across.

'Do you mind then if I read a few things out from this? I've marked the pages with slips of paper.'

Ned's eyes narrowed.

'Just how long have you been planning this?' he said with suspicion.

'Only since I've become marooned on Ice Planet Midwinter' she laughed and then opened the first page.

'Christmas' she read out, 'was always preceded by the singing of carols and festive songs. From Anglo-Saxon times, Wassailing was common, where people danced and sang. They shouted Wassail, from the Norse, 'Waes Hael', meaning 'Be of good health.'

She looked up, remembering they had all said Wassail before their dinner.

'But you know about that, don't you?'

She went on.

'The toast was used to waken the earth and trees to encourage the spirits into ensuring a good harvest in the next year. It was originally performed on the Twelfth Night of Yule. Basically though, and these are your great-grandmother's words, it was just an excellent excuse for singing, dancing and drinking.

'Later, the poor people of the parish would sing at the doors of the local gentry in the hope of being thrown some coins while the residents of the big houses were in a benevolent mood. More often than not, they would also be given a warm alcoholic drink and a mince pie if they were lucky, before they went on their way.

'The singing of carols usually took place, at least since Victorian times, around a Christmas tree with a member of the family playing the piano.'

She moved towards the door.

'Follow me' she said, so they did with no questions. She felt like the Pied Piper.

'Now, I don't know if our local gentry is feeling benevolent,' she grinned at Ned who gave a gracious and benevolent bow, 'but we do have a Christmas tree.'

She opened the front door

'In fact, we have two.'

They all moved on to the top step of the porch and then down the three steps onto the cleared path, so they all had a good view of the second White Pine opposite the far dining room window. That was spectacularly lit up as well.

'Beautiful' breathed Mrs H and there were murmurs of agreement from everyone.

'Just like old times' said Rose, staring at the trees, perfectly silhouetted against the night sky, the lights like stars that had lent a bit of sparkle to the trees for Christmas.

Bridie risked a sideways look at Ned. He was looking at the display in wonder. The lantern above the porch seemed to be casting a mellow glow in his eyes. At least that's what she thought it was. He didn't say a word but he looked happy- and that was what mattered. There were a few moments of blissful silence rudely interrupted by Mrs H.

'I hope you're not expecting us to go and sing carols under those trees, young lady?'

The spell was broken and everyone laughed.

'Not under the trees- no...' Bridie replied.

There was a groan from Ned.

'- but perhaps a couple while we're standing here on this beautiful starlit, snowy and absolutely freezing cold evening, I thought we'd start with- 'We Wish You a Merry Christmas? Just the first verse. I'm sure you can manage that, Ned.'

'I'll try.' he said 'The effort might keep me warm.'

'Wimp' she said 'I thought you were the hardy, outdoor type?'

'I am when I'm working or moving.'

'Well go for a run around the trees while you're singing' Bridie suggested while everyone laughed at the exchange. Ned too, luckily.

Bridie started the singing off and soon they were all belting it out at the top of their voices. Tam and Tink came dashing through at this rude interruption to their sleep. They seemed to be convinced that the humans were being attacked by wild animals, judging by the noise they were making.

'Now, how about 'Oh Come All Ye Faithful?'

'My favourite carol' said Mrs H.

At this point, Marcus slipped away towards his flat. He didn't have much of a voice, he thought, but he could make music in another way. Zinnia noticed him go and smiled at him.

The carol sounded lovely, carrying across the snowy landscape and echoing in the big empty space around them. Ned's and Henry's voices were a warm, bass sound contrasting with the women's voices.

'Right' said Bridie when they'd finished. 'What shall we sing next?'

'You said a couple' complained Ned but he was smiling, along with the rest of them. Just then, Marcus came around the corner of the Hall. In his hand, he carried a violin. As he approached them, he lifted up his other hand which carried the bow, put the violin under his chin and started playing a carol. He played the first verse and chorus of 'It Came Upon a Midnight Clear' while they all stood enthralled at the delicate melodic sounds. The notes seemed to spiral upwards as though reaching to heaven. When he had finished he looked over at Zinnia who went over to stand next to him. The violin started up again, but this time, Zinnia joined in, singing the words in a confident way. Bridie remembered that Mrs H had told her that she and her husband had sung folk songs together.

'Join in' said Zinnia, so they did.

Everyone looked happy as they turned to go back inside.

'What about finishing on an upbeat one?' Bridie said loudly. Somehow she didn't want it to finish.

'My toes are freezing' moaned Mrs H 'unless you want *me* to run around the Christmas tree to warm up too?'

She looked sideways at Bridie and everyone laughed.

Marcus took advantage of this by playing a few notes on his violin, which Bridie recognised.

'Deck the halls!' she shouted, laughing.

He started the intro again and it was one of those carols that you couldn't help joining in with.

'Deck the halls with boughs of holly, fa la la la la, la la la laaah'

They sang lustily while Marcus stamped one foot to the beat.

Bridie grabbed Ned on impulse and linked one arm, turning him round in a circle. Then they linked the other arms and did the same. Of course, this set Tam and Tink into a frenzy. They did their own dance comprising of jumping up at the dancers, turning round in circles and barking their own version of the song.

Laughing, Ned went up to fetch Mrs H who didn't even protest. Soon they were all swirling around on the path and swapping partners with each other as they formed a circle. Zinnia, Henry and Rose had joined in while Marcus loudly kept the beat with his foot.

They were all red-faced either with the cold or the dancing - and on the final. 'Fa la la la la, la la la LAAAH!' everyone collapsed with their hands on their knees, out of breath with the effort. They were all shrieking with laughter though, so Bridie considered it a job well done. Christmas had finally returned to Midwinter Hall.

Chapter 25

Games and More Food

The rest of the Christmas festivities degenerated from there - in a good way. Bridie thought it was due in part to the exhilaration of having a real Christmas again, but she had to admit that a lot of it was due to the influence of Mrs H and Rose's. 'I don't think they're *that* alcoholic, young man' homemade wines.

Mrs H presented them with an elderberry wine to warm them all up when they went back inside. By this time, Ned had already got his guitar out and was playing a few Christmas songs. After one of Rose's blackcurrant and apple wines, the songs degenerated into, 'All I want for Christmas is my Two Front Teeth' which nevertheless, everyone joined in with at the top of their voices.

As another of the bottles was placed on the table, the party found that they were laughing but didn't quite know what at. The last offering was Slade's 'Well Here It Is, Merry Christmas, Everybody's Having Fun' sung at a deafening noise level and accompanied by a manic Ned and Marcus on guitar and violin respectively, with Ned treating his acoustic guitar as though it were electric. Bridie wondered hazily if he practised air guitar in his bedroom.

The dogs, who narrowly avoided covering their ears with their paws, were trying to sleep in front of the fire, against all odds, with one eye on Ned's feet as he danced around. After this, they all collapsed on various comfortable chairs, except Mrs H, who got straight up again.

'If I sit down properly, I'll never get up and I need to get your Christmas supper.'

'Supper?' was repeated in amazement by Bridie until she realised that despite the huge dinner, she was peckish again after all.

*

Fifteen minutes later - after discussing the merits of folk rock (Marcus), rock ballads (Ned), traditional folk. (Zinnia), followed by. ' You can't beat a bit of Acker Bilk' (Henry) and then 'I don't care as long as I can dance to it' from Bridie. (You could dance to the National

Anthem') Ned had replied - Mrs H and Rose called them through.

The table was once again groaning with all manner of delicious food. A huge pork pie glistening with a savoury glaze. There were little puff pastry parcels with spiced meat in them, knobbly cheese straws and of course turkey sandwiches and ham sandwiches. For afterwards there was trifle or buttered apple tart with a bowl full of whipped cream to accompany it.

Everyone looked at each other and patted their stomachs as they saw it, but soon they had made great inroads into the feast. At least it would soak some of the alcohol up.

'Shall I open some more wine?' asked Ned half-heartedly, anticipating the answer.

Everyone agreed instead that a coffee afterwards was just the ticket and Zinnia helped Bridie to get them ready. Just before they took them through, Zinnia leaned across to the younger woman.

'Thank you for this. I know you did it primarily for Ned- but you made time to come and fetch me- and you know I'm as stubborn as Ned is. It could have been awkward but it hasn't been at all and I've enjoyed myself immensely. So here's to you, you wonderful girl. You've certainly shaken this place up.'

Zinnia pulled her in for a hug as they laughed. They both knew it was Ned who had been shaken up - the others were just waiting for him to come round. Zinnia wondered how long it would have taken if Bridie hadn't come to work here. Mind you, she hadn't helped matters either. She put her head down and looked thoughtful until the rattle of coffee cups on Bridie's tray brought her round.

*

'Next' said Bridie as they sat in the dining room with their coffees and stared dreamily through at the Christmas tree, 'old Gertrude says…'

Ned tutted at this slight to his illustrious ancestor but spoilt it with a grin.

'… Old Gertrude says' Bridie went on 'that parlour games are played for the guest's delight.'

'I can't move' said Mrs H simply.

'You don't have to, we can do it from our seats. Standing is optional if it helps.'

'Helps what?' Ned asked suspiciously.

'Who am I?'

'You're Bridie' he said without missing a beat. 'Surely you haven't forgotten.' She stuck her tongue out at him. 'But don't you need headbands or stickers for that game?'

'Not the way we play it. It's simple. Someone picks a famous person for you - the one who picks can't join in the game - but it works out evenly in the end. I've sort of changed the rules so I'm hoping they work out.'

'I don't think I can... I mean, what do you do?' Henry wasn't keen on games apart from dominos.

'Pick one for Henry can you Rose? One that he'll know. Write it on this memo pad and show it to him, then he's just got to act it out till one of us gets it. Remember Rose, you can't play for this round, as there are no famous people already written down for us.'

Bridie passed over the memo pad she'd found on a side table in the hallway and Rose scribbled something down. A few seconds later, Henry sprung into life, patting an imaginary hat, smoking a pretend fat cigar, and making his features into a particularly sulky Bulldog and if that wasn't enough, he stuck two fingers up. The victory sign, of course, this being Henry. Everyone shouted out at once but Mrs H just pipped everyone to it by shouting 'Churchill!' The others each had their go until finally, there were only Ned and Bridie left.

'My turn' shouted Bridie and wrote a name down, showing it to Ned. If she was hoping to embarrass him, which she was, she was quite wrong as he embraced his inner Dolly Parton completely.

He got up from his chair and strutted up and down, then grabbed a couple of oranges to shove up his jumper. Nobody could answer for laughing. It was a long time since they'd seen him like this. A fun person.

'Mae West' shouted Henry.

'Nobody'll know who Mae West is' said Rose, nudging him in the ribs. He carried on.

'What do you call that woman, Kim Kalashnikov or somebody?' This produced loud laughter.

Mrs H tried to speak but doubled over with laughter herself, as Bridie made a muffled snort.

'No, not one of the Kalashnikovs' spluttered Ned.

'Shush you're not allowed to talk' said Rose.

He mimed bouffant long hair, someone over a foot shorter than him- and finally after 'Brigitte Bardot' from Henry, he mimed singing.

'Dolly Parton' screamed Zinnia as everyone said that they were just going to guess that too.

Now, there was only Bridie left. She looked in trepidation at Ned who was smiling viciously as he wrote. And there was the name in front of her. Baron Albrecht Von Richthofen- the Red Baron. She gave him a 'look'. Well, if he could embrace it, so could she.

She stood up and pointed at her hair. She then put imaginary flying goggles on using her hands to make the shape. Then she grabbed hold of a non-existence joystick and started flying around the room. She wasn't allowed to make aeroplane noises so she put her arms out, tilting them from side to side. She 'flew' up close behind them and when no one got it, mostly through being rendered unable to speak, she threw caution to the wind and started making aeroplane noises. This is when the dogs joined in the game and followed her round, jumping up every few seconds.

When Ned began to weakly protest in sign language, she picked up a clean ladle and pointed it at him, making phut phut engine noises and then BOOM bombing noises. He immediately picked up a large unused serving spoon and bombed her back with louder sound effects.

Rose and Henry were almost crying on each other's shoulders and Mrs H nearly collapsed onto the remains of her apple tart. Marcus was quietly chuckling, his shoulders going up and down and Zinnia, desperate as her competitive spirit was to get the answer, couldn't spit her guesses out for laughing.

'Do you give up?' Bridie said.

'Yes!' came the chorus.

'It's the Red Baron, Baron Von Richthofen. I win!' she said dancing round as Ned threw serviettes at her.

'Oh my goodness' said Mrs H after a couple of minutes of recovery, 'I'd better get this table cleared before it's used to reenact the Battle of Trafalgar.'

'I'll help' said Bridie immediately.

'And I'll get out port and brandy in the sitting room for anyone who can manage it.'

It seemed that this long, happy day hadn't ended yet. So when everything was cleared, Bridie chose to announce the next thing in Gertrude's book.

'While we're all sitting in front of the Yule log we as our ancestors did, we can think what Christmas story we are going to tell. '

Ned squeezed his eyes shut.

'Gertie says that the Christmas tales told were usually ghost stories. So you can choose those or something entirely different.'

She looked at Henry's face - and Marcus looked worried too.

'It needn't be long. Just a snippet of something you know about Christmas, or something you know about Midwinter - or anything really.'

They all looked thoughtful, searching in their minds for their stories as their faces were lit up by the brightness of the flames.

Chapter 26

Stories around the fire.

They were all seated around the great hearth. The fire was burning brightly but the lights were low. Ned had left the lamps on which shone with a mellow golden light but had turned the overhead lights off. As a result, it seemed like they had gone back in time, beyond the Christmas of today and towards the Yule festivals of old, as people sat around their fires telling stories full of wonder, legend and mysticism. Passing their stories down from village to village, from generation to generation.

Ned, poked at the fire, still burning steadily - and a few sparks flew out towards them. Tam and Tink looked up in alarm and drew back, Tam to sit on Ned's feet and Tink to stare at Bridie in disdain before deciding the sparks weren't really her fault and settling on her feet instead.

'Who is going to be first?' asked Zinnia.

She was enjoying this Christmas rather more than she liked to admit. She *had* been very lonely but things were feeling better now in every way.

There was a silence that usually Bridie would have filled, but the truth was, she had no idea of what story she could tell. Eventually, Mrs H spoke.

'I suppose it'll be me then?' she asked rhetorically, 'I can't really think of a Christmas ghost story as such. Let me see.' She settled her chubby hands on her lap.

*

'When Kenneth and I first came here, we were told not to go up to the Sacred Wood. That's what Ned's father called it, but I've heard it called Silent Wood and Druid's Wood too. Silent is a good name, for that's just what it is. Nothing seems to move, nothing seems to exist but I'm sure it must as the trees look healthy enough.

'Now, depending on whom you talked to, it was 'haunted by ghosts', it was 'sacred to the ancient druids' or it was 'a holy place, sacred to God'. Many of the older workers at that time thought that it was inhabited by fairies. The little folk. They thought that if you ventured in there, you would get spirited away to Fairyland.

'Some of the cynics later, amongst the younger ones, said that there was another reason they wanted to keep us out. A murder and a buried corpse, perhaps. There was no doubt though that there was a strange atmosphere, whatever the truth of it was. I've never dared step inside and not only because I've been told not to. I've never been tempted but I have stuck my nose in there and, I could swear that the air itself changed.

'In those days the festival of Midwinter was celebrated here just as much as Christmas. Candles were lit in every window and on every table to keep the light burning in the darkness of the shorter days.

'So it's not a ghost story exactly but the ghost - or the spirit of Midwinter, lives in that silent wood. I, for one, believe that.

*

Mrs H nodded to show that she had finished and relaxed back in her chair. Bridie was amazed that this solid practical woman believed there was something strange in the wood. Rose sat up.

'My turn' she said, shuffling to the edge of her chair and putting her hands together as if starting a recitation.

*

'I've heard many stories of that wood over the years and I've lived here longer than any of you around this table now. My father was the groom when they kept horses and me and my family lived in the cottage where Henry and I still live. My father and his family before him had lived in these parts forever. He was deeply rooted in the tradition of both this place and the countryside surrounding it.

'He told me – and he believed it – that the wood was inhabited by tree nymphs and sprites. Fairy-like creatures. They protected the oakwood itself. The most important of these sprites, he said, was a Queen or a goddess called Deri. D.E.R.I. is how it's spelt'

Here Bridie gasped and everyone turned to look at her. She said nothing but turned to look at Ned, who looked guilty. She had mentioned that very name, phonetically at least, on Midwinter's Eve and he had pretended not to know it. After a few seconds of hesitation, Rose went on.

'Deri protected the wood itself and the land around it. The tree sprites were rooted to a place and my father said this included Midwinter Hall itself. She is also supposed to protect the people who live and work here and the animals on the land. She is here forever looking after us all.

'You may all think that sounds daft and I'm not given to stupid fancies myself but, I don't know, I believe in her. I've been in the wood when I was younger– so, yes, I believe in her.'

Bridie, even though she couldn't turn her attention away from Rose, caught Zinnia's expression in her peripheral vision and knew that her own face reflected it. Did everyone believe in Deri? Rose went on.

'Some people over the years have said that they've seen her but my father didn't believe them as they couldn't describe her or their descriptions varied as they couldn't remember properly I believed them though as I knew they were honest people.

'They call her the Midwinter Spirit because the first time she appears is on Midwinter's Eve, the winter solstice of December 21st and she goes on for the full twelve days until New Year's Day. She stays there, according to my dad, until the next year and forever after but no one sees her. She's there though, quiet and invisible, for the rest of the time, protecting the wood and Midwinter Hall.

*

Henry jumped in straight away, probably to get it over with or just possibly because he needed to say something to a certain person.

'I haven't got much to say except that I believe in the legend of the wood. Apart from anything else, it changed my life for the better.

'I came to this estate as a young lad, not long after I'd left school. I'd started a job in town but I wanted to follow in my father's footsteps. He worked in public gardens and I wanted to work with my hands in the earth too. Seeing new life peeping through it.

'During winter, a month or so after I started here, I was sent to the holly grove. I collected some holly and took it back but then at the last minute was sent for some mistletoe. I trailed back up there. I reached up and grabbed a bunch at the edge of the holly wood and when I looked across to the Silent Wood, I saw a glow, part of the way down, next to the path.

'I knew I wasn't supposed to but I went in and it was then that I first saw Rose. She was sixteen then. She was looking up at a tree that seemed as though it was lit from the inside. I didn't know what it was but, believe it or not, I didn't much care at that moment. Something else more important had captured my attention.

'I went up to her, we looked into each other's eyes and fell in love immediately. Everything just seemed to fall into place because I realised I was still holding the mistletoe, so I lifted it above our heads and snatched a kiss. We got married two years later. From that moment onwards we were inseparable just like we are now.

*

At this point, Henry and Rose looked at each other with such love in their eyes that Bridie was sure she wasn't the only one fighting back tears.

Marcus spoke into the silence.

*

'I haven't got anything to say about Midwinter as I lived nearly forty miles away and I have only been here around six years. I will say this though, I wouldn't dismiss anything unexplained because I know from experience that not everything *has* an explanation.

'Before... Before my marriage broke up, we lived in a remote cottage, a short walk from a small inaccessible lake. We used to see lights down by the lakeside on a night. Eventually, I went down to investigate, keeping really quiet and found – well, I still don't know what I found. Wisps perhaps? Not little Willo' the wisps but human-sized ones with only an outline showing - or like smoke in the rough shape of a body. There were a few of them giving off a strange light. They were either floating or darting a few feet above the water. After a while, they seemed to accept me and came nearer to me around the lake edge.

'I tried my hardest over the next few days to find a scientific explanation for it because I considered myself a rational person but nothing was right. Nothing fitted.

'One night, my wife followed me. Took it into her head that I'd been meeting another woman and the lights were our torches. What she saw scared the living daylights out of her. She spent the whole night sitting up with all the lights on while I tried to tell her that we'd move as soon as we could if that's what she wanted. It was no good. She packed the next day and left the cottage.

It was for the best, she had been unfaithful before and soon found someone else. We had grown apart. Whereas I could accept what I saw, she would never have an accepting mind or be willing to understand that there must be more to our world than we will ever know.

*

Not only had Marcus never spoken for so long but it was the first time he had discussed his wife and especially her leaving. The other man came later then but it seemed that now, he was more than ready to move on. Bridie was even more surprised at his admission of a belief in the supernatural. Was she the only one who was a sceptic? Yet, after all that had happened to her, could she really say she didn't believe anymore?

Zinnia nodded at Marcus and then looked at Bridie and Ned. When neither of them offered to go next, she went on.

Chapter 27

More Stories

Zinnia began.

*

'I have always believed in the supernatural and its possibilities. We were very into seances and Ouija boards when we were young and very spiritual when we were new-age hippies in Wales.

'As we got older, Emlyn surprised me by wanting to move away from the Welsh mountains to a gentler pasture as we weren't getting any younger. Emlyn had a gift - he could sense things, so when he fell for this house in the Yorkshire Wolds straight away, I didn't question it. He said it was one of the most spiritual places he'd been, he could feel it. He said it was due to the wood at the bottom of - of *the* land.

'He spent some time in there, although he tried not to disturb it too much and he said that dryads were living in the trees. This coming from anyone else might have sounded like he was, 'having an episode' but I knew him enough to understand that if he said it, he meant it. He called it a sacred wood because he had researched it and there was a possibility it was on an ancient processional way that the druids used to walk along on their way to worship there.

'We didn't mention this to you Ned as we weren't sure how you felt about it. You seem to be a practical, logical sort of chap and besides you'd not long lost your father.

'When Emlyn was diagnosed, he went into decline fairly quickly, both his body and his mind. One day he got up, stronger than he'd felt in a while. I was hopeful - but he shook his head. He walked slowly down to the wood and wouldn't let me go with him to help him.

'When he came back he was exhausted but smiling, happy for the first time in a long while. He hugged me and sat me down. He said that Deri was in the woods. Deri, he told me, like the name of the river in Wales. Although he hadn't seen her properly, he saw the light from the tree. He felt her hands on his head and then on his shoulders- and he said the heat went through him and he could now feel no pain.

'I asked if that was because he was getting better. He answered me, saying he thought the opposite was true. We spent the day looking at our old photos and reading our old diaries - laughing at things we had almost forgotten.

'Before we went to bed he said to me 'Promise me if you ever feel alone, go to the wood. You will find what you need there.' I nodded as there didn't seem anything to say. I didn't want to ask any questions as I didn't want the answers, although I found great solace in following his advice later.

'We slept that night, wrapped in each other's arms. In the morning, he had passed on.'

*

The whole room was quiet. Nobody wanted to interrupt the silence. Eventually, Tam came up to Zinnia and put a paw on her lap while staring at her with compassionate, amber eyes. This broke the spell and Zinnia reached down and held her, her tears running into her soft, black and white coat. She gathered herself together.

'Now Ned, Midwinter Hall is yours. Surely you have some tales to tell?'

*

Bridie's left eyebrow raised slightly as the thoughts came into her head that Zinnia had been right. He was too logical to give much credence to the beliefs of his workers. She wondered if he had known that they felt this way. Yet there had been the non-religious 'Grace' - and the Wassail - and- why had he lied to her? The answer was about to be revealed as Ned spoke.

*

'Firstly, I owe Bridie an apology. When she told me about something she'd seen in the woods, I tried to dismiss it. She didn't appear to think there was anything strange about what she'd seen, so I carried on letting her think that. She was only here to catalogue the books before she left again- and I didn't want to worry her unnecessarily. I regret not taking her into my confidence now.

'As for being practical, Zinnia, I would agree that I am. That practicality has made me test every other explanation for the phenomena in the wood before I came to the. 'Logical' conclusion, like Marcus, that there *was* no explanation.

'Among the leather-bound books in the library, Bridie, are two volumes, written by my great-grandfather, Roland Fynch-Stratton,

Gertrude's husband. In the first, he documents folklore and superstitions of the whole of Yorkshire. In the second, he writes of a more localised area around here, most of it given up to the Midwinter area. He also wrote a book called 'The Ancient Trackways of the Yorkshire Wolds.'

'This is when he came to the same conclusion as Emrys. He said that our wood was sacred, being on an ancient trackway. It was a ceremonial path, a processional way that led the druids to the sacred grove and others on the route. Roland says that it wasn't just the arrival at the grove that was important to the druids but the feeling, the awareness, of the country around them as they journeyed.

'My father was a devotee of these books and urged me to read them. He was very proud of the ancient traditions carried out in this valley and its surrounds. He firmly believed in our 'Midwinter Spirit' of the Silent Wood, as he too had felt what most of you have felt. As for who I think Deri is, there are many answers to that, mostly from Roland's books. Most are speculation but some are more possible than others. The Fae are supposed to be elementals taking on forms of earth, water, fire and wind at will, so they could, if you were to believe this, take on the form of a tree.

'In his book, Roland says that dryads were supposed to have olive green skin and wear wreaths of leaves in their hair. The name dryads is where druids were supposed to get their name from. Deri, I suppose came from the same word group, as Duir was a letter from the ancient druid Ogham alphabet, meaning 'oak' and Deru means 'knower of the truth.' Everything, including the implied name Deri, seems to derive from the majestic Oak.

'I have always respected our... I don't call them tales, I call it our history. Especially when I found out that Midwinter Hall is named after our Midwinter Spirit and not the other way around. It was just Fynch's Farm before it was rebuilt in a grander manner and renamed Midwinter Hall. Although the whole area around here was known as Midwinter. We felt special as she was in our wood. And before you say anything Zinnia, I know all woodland should belong to everyone. You must agree though that, although this tree Spirit looks after us, we look after the wood in return and make sure it is not damaged in any way. Being a sacred wood doesn't just mean 'holy', it means 'entitled to reveration and respect'- and we try to carry that out.

'My own belief in the spirit of the oak was made absolute on the day my father died.'

Everyone seemed to be holding their breath at this announcement and in the back of Bridie's mind, a bell rang to highlight the recent conversation they had in front of the sitting room fire.

'It's common knowledge that I had words with my father before he died. He wasn't himself because of the medication and the illness. To compound everything, I expect I was behaving like a spoilt, rejected child. I left him and went out angrily, walking quickly, although I didn't know where to. I was thinking to myself that I would give him a few days to calm down before I saw him again. The doctor had said he could last like this until summer and his temper was getting worse all the time.

'I found myself in the Silent Wood. surprised at how I'd got there. I walked softly onward until I saw a diffused light just back from the trackway and stopped, turning to look at it. I felt, not heard, a voice in my head. 'Go home now. Go home. Go!'

'It managed to sound calm yet extremely urgent at the same time. A woman's voice. It didn't stop until I turned and ran as fast as I ever have. I collected my sister from the hallway and ran to my father's bedroom with her.

'He had taken a turn for the worse but, conversely, was almost back to his old self. We managed to say everything we needed to say and we made our peace. He knew he was leaving that day and we knew it too. He died not long after.

'Yet even though we parted friends, I have let it colour my enjoyment of Christmas ever since. That is of course until this year.'

*

He stopped here and smiled at everyone and they responded with smiles of understanding. He didn't need to say any more.

'Well, that's my story. Now there's only Bridie and this should be a good one' he laughed.

Everyone looked at Bridie expectantly. They knew they were in for a laugh as usual. She swallowed and looked down, shaking her head slightly. They gradually began to realise that Bridie hadn't been herself through all the stories. No interruptions, no sarcastic remarks, no making light of things. She had become quieter after each story until now it seemed she had lost her voice altogether.

'Bridie?' whispered Ned, a concerned frown on his face. She looked up.

'No. I mean no I don't want to tell a story. There's nothing to tell.'

'From what you told me there's plenty to…' started Ned.

'No, I was mistaken.' She made to get up. 'Does anyone want another drink? Coffee? Hot chocolate? I could do with a brandy...'

'Bridie!' Ned spoke louder this time and put a hand on her arm. Mrs H who was sitting opposite her looked her in the eyes.

'Tell your story girl. Whatever it is, we will listen.'

'You won't believe me' she muttered.

'Look at me.' said Mrs H and so Bridie did. 'We know you as a very honest girl, sometimes too honest. If it's important to you that we all believe you, then let me assure you, we will.'

Bridie took a sip of the brandy that Ned handed to her and said,

'Perhaps I'd better swear on Roland Fynch-Stratton's book that I am telling the truth, the whole truth and nothing but the truth - because after hearing your stories, mine differs in quite a substantial way.'

Chapter 28

Bridie's story

'Let me start by saying that, before I came here, I wasn't a believer. In much at all really. In Christianity or any other religions. I didn't believe political freedom existed and I wasn't sure about personal freedom either. I didn't believe in the concept of true love - for me at least. I didn't believe in the supernatural, in all its guises. Along with everything else, I would have been happy to believe it existed but I needed proof. I am a sceptic and a cynic- but if any of the things I said I didn't believe in could be proved then I would be happy to accept it. Nothing had been proved so I remained a sceptic.

'Someone once said that believing in something without definite proof that it exists is the very definition of faith. If so, then I'm not sure I believe in faith either. Hope, yes- but it's not the same as blind faith.

'However, my scepticism has been severely shaken since I arrived here, especially because of the way my experience differs slightly from yours.

'I walked into the Silent Wood on Midwinter's Eve. It shows the extent to which the mystic or pagan areas of life affected me by the fact that I had no idea it even *was* Midwinter's Eve or the solstice or what they meant.

'The first indication something was different was that Tam and Tink wouldn't go into the wood. They didn't seem scared, more in awe. It felt like they were keeping guard up at the entrance. It's what happened next that you may find hard to believe and why I didn't want to tell you about it.

'Just after this point, because of Ned's reply that it was probably the young lady belonging to the Rushtons' Farm, my scepticism was still to the fore, to the extent that I was laughing at myself at almost believing that Deri was a ghost.'

Bridie told them all about her first encounter with Deri as a young girl. There were no interruptions, just wide-eyed attention, so she went on.

'The next time I saw her was just after I had found out that Ned had lied to me about the existence of Deri. Even so, I wanted to prove that seeing this... whatever she was, didn't happen. Then I would have to start thinking of a rational explanation as to what happened. It could have got quite complicated.

'This time after failing to find her and then watching a beautiful Christmas Eve sunset, I turned around to see the glowing tree. It had moved – it was in the middle of the wood. I am not kidding you, as ridiculous as it sounds. What's more, Deri, when I saw her, was no longer a teenage girl but a young woman. She was without doubt the same person. I felt calm in her presence.

'She still talked to me- or so I thought, until she herself questioned it and gave me doubts. It was then I realised that the few words she had spoken, weren't actually spoken out loud - although I could 'hear' them in my mind just as much as if she had. Her expression echoed the thought she sent to me - but her lips didn't move.

'This shook me to the core. This was something that couldn't be faked. Unless I was imagining it all of course or had unknowingly taken some hallucinogenic substance, which was nearly as unlikely as the scenario I found myself in.

'The next and so far, the last time that I saw her was this morning- and she didn't speak to me. Yet this morning made me believe more than ever before.

'I took Bessie to collect Zinnia as I thought it might persuade her to come to Christmas dinner. Even though Ned had mentioned tying her up at the edge of the wood, I still hoped she might go through. Normally, of course, being an animal, Bessie wouldn't have entered the Silent Wood. I still don't understand why that should be but I respect the higher senses of animals.

'When Bessie stopped and wouldn't move, I started to tie her to the lower branch of an oak tree which was overhanging the track. Suddenly, she looked up and saw something that made her want to go in. As we walked slowly down the path through the Silent Wood she turned towards the large oak, which wasn't as luminescent as before.

'This time there was no figure next to the tree but one inside it, instead. Deri's top half reached out of the tree to Bessie and stretched her arms to,…I want to say stroke her nose but she didn't touch her. Her hands hovered just above, with light cascading down onto Bessie, who seemed to bow before her - and I just knew the horse was feeling this wonderful radiant heat just as we all have.

'We continued down the path. Zinnia was already on her way to the wood and – well, here she is with us all today. So as you can see, my faith has emerged fully fledged. I now have to say I believe in the supernatural if that is what this is. Spirituality, mysticism, the unknown - call it what you will. I now have proof that I believe in one of those things I didn't believe in before. What's more, I feel that I shouldn't have needed proof - that it cheapens what it is, whatever that may be. Phenomena connected to Nature in some different way, unrelated to how we humans connect with it? It's something that I now feel has been here for much longer than any of us and I feel that I should inherently and without any doubts, have understood that.

' I do now.'

Chapter 29

Side by Side

There was a silence that lasted only a few moments before Rose said,

'It has been heard of before Bridie but it is very rare. You are privileged and I think that it makes you special. There's some reason that things have moved in this way. You just don't know it yet.'

Bridie gave her a watery smile and Mrs H came across to her, pulling her up for one of her comforting hugs.

'I knew when you were asking about the Rushton's granddaughter, that you had seen Deri. Especially when you rushed off to the woods straight afterwards.'

Ned, who had been sitting next to her, reached for her hand and looked up at her with clear, honest eyes.

'We believe you Bridie. It's taken a lot for you to admit it all but you are a very honest person. I should know. I have been on the receiving end of your blunt honesty many times.'

He grinned and the atmosphere lightened immediately.

'My mother was like you, according to my father. She couldn't let herself believe properly. I think because she came from Norway, she thought that everything supernatural was inherently evil and something to be feared. All those Norse tales of one-eyed monsters, fearsome trolls, dark elves and evil wolves. So she chose to disparage it.

'My father tried in vain to say that the trees and beings in the wood that protected us were only ever a force for good. He never succeeded. So I'm very pleased that you have accepted this. It's much better than fighting it and it will open you up to so much more.'

There were more questions and answers and then a special hot chocolate before most of the Christmas guests went out into the cold. The stories had sobered them up and the long day was catching up with them. Bridie saw Ned pour a fortifying sip of something alcoholic into a silver and leather hip flask on the drinks tray.

'We're going to have to get off home now - Rose can hardly keep her eyes open, see' said Henry and they all turned to look at her. She dug him in the ribs again and they both laughed.

'It was *you* who was nodding off, you old devil' she said.

'Before everyone leaves, I have something I want to say.'

Zinnia suddenly looked serious. Ned looked worried. Surely she wasn't going to mention the top field today?

'Ned, I still don't want the wood disturbed by twice daily trampings through it - even if you can get the donkeys to enter it, which I doubt.'

Oh no, thought Bridie, please, just leave it for now.

'What's more, I think you agree with me and wouldn't do it if you had a choice. Yet the choice is there and has always been mine. I was just too pig-headed to see it. So, if you wouldn't mind giving the donkeys up....'

Now everyone was looking upset. How could she change so quickly?

'I would like to take them instead.'

Everyone let their breath out and now looked relieved but Ned was undecided. He had been looking forward to having the donkeys on his land, safe and sound. He looked like he was going to refuse.

'I think that sounds like a good idea' intervened Bridie, while Mrs H nodded almost imperceptibly at her, 'but where would you keep them?'

'I was hoping it would be the top or bottom field- or our field, as I hope we can call it now until proof turns up, if it ever does. You can visit whenever you want but I will pay for their food and upkeep and will be happy to. I love all animals, although you may be forgiven for thinking that I don't.

'The brick outbuilding near my house needs clearing and cleaning to make it suitable for their indoor stabling but - if you can put the Donkey Sanctuary off for a little while - I'm sure I can manage it. Marcus says he'll help.'

'We'll all help' Ned said enthusiastically, obviously coming round to the idea. 'With you. Marcus, me, Bridie and Henry, we can get the job done in no time. I've got hay and food ready here for them which will last a couple of weeks or more. When they can get the donkeys through, I'll bring it round in the truck and trailer.'

'And what's wrong with Mrs H and Rose helping too?' exclaimed Mrs H, hands on hips.

'Not exactly little delicate, wilting flowers are we?'

There was laughter as they had to agree. Tam and Tink danced round them as if they wanted to help too - but everyone knew their definition of help was a lot looser than everyone else's. Marcus spoke.

'Maybe tomorrow? To clear the shed? It looks like it's thawing out there.'

They all rushed to the window and found the candlelight was reflecting back at them, so they opened the front door instead.

'It's right' said Henry. 'Nearly all the snow's off the upper branches. A few bare patches here and there too. Gritter might be able to get to these parts now.' Everyone looked thrilled.

Everyone that is, except Bridie and Ned, who exchanged brief looks. Bridie quickly looked away, hoping he couldn't read her expression - but hadn't his been the same?

*

"Oh we ain't got a barrel of money, maybe we're ragged and funny, but we'll travel along, singing this song, side by side."

Henry, Rose, Bridie and Ned had almost reached Rose Cottage. They had all linked arms, supposedly to hold each other up if they came across an icy patch, though Bridie suspected this just meant all four of them would fall at the same time.

The mere act of them all walking down the path in a line, side by side, was enough to set Henry and Rose off chuckling. They started singing with Ned and Bridie joining in, kicking their legs up with every beat. This made it even more likely that they would all end up in a heap on the ground, but nobody seemed worried.

Bridie suspected that the 'special' hot chocolate made to fortify them against the cold had a good percentage of alcohol added. Or maybe they were just all happy. The two residents of Rose Cottage certainly seemed to be and after profuse thanks for a wonderful day, they all hugged each other tightly - with Ned saying it would happen again next year. Then the two of them stood arm in arm on their doorstep, waving Bridie and Ned off until they disappeared from sight.

*

They had told Mrs H earlier, to go up to her flat with a sherry and leave whatever washing up was left, to them.

'Sherry? I'll be asleep if I have any more alcohol' she chuntered good-naturedly.

'Isn't going to sleep what you normally do at this late hour?' Bridie had asked.

Mrs H had looked from one to the other.

'If you insist then and only because I've recorded a Midsomer Murders Christmas special. I've had a right grand time, Ned, thank you - and thanks to you of course Bridie. I've never known anyone so full of ideas - and the 'front' to carry them out.'

They had both hugged Mrs H who was too tired to look embarrassed but her smile was wide and happy.

*

Tam and Tink had come to Rose Cottage with them, running ahead to keep out of the way of the mad foursome coming down the track. They were now waiting at the top greenhouse. As soon as Bridie and Ned reached them, they ran off, past the front door of the Hall, past the far lantern-lit White Pine and then headed across towards the track leading to the woods.

'Looks like they want another walk?' she grinned at Ned.

'I was taking them anyway. We have a visit to make, you and I.'

Bridie accepted this without question, despite it being nearly midnight. She rather liked the idea of 'you and I'.

Chapter 30

Wassail!

There was no doubt a thaw had set in. They could see drops of melted snow falling from the branches as they moved up the trackway. It was still cold enough to see their breath coming out as vapour in front of them- but there was a definite change in the air.

'Do you think the gritter will get through to here?' asked Bridie, not knowing whether she would be happy or sad if it did.

'Possibly, although I think that Charlie Rushton will get the snow plough out, now that Christmas Day is over. They'll be having their Boxing Day party and they'll want it fairly clear for incoming relatives.'

'Including their granddaughter?' she asked cheekily.

'Including Leyla' he smiled ruefully.

'So I suppose I'll be able to go home then?'

She saw his head turn quickly towards her but then he faced the front again. After a moment he said,

'I wouldn't want you to risk it in that small car of yours. It would be bad enough with an all-terrain vehicle.'

'Mmm,' she said and smiled to herself while he wasn't looking.

The dogs had reached the top and had settled to wait at the entrance to the Silent Wood as usual.

'Why do you think animals won't go in? I mean, dogs and donkeys and horses are part of Nature too- and it doesn't seem right to keep them out.'

Ned took a while to answer by which time they had reached Tam and Tink.

'They are never kept out. They have gone in once or twice of their own volition - like Bessie did with you earlier. It's almost as if they were being called for some reason. The main reason I suppose that they stay here is that animal senses are almost on a different plane to ours. They can feel things within the wood that they have great respect for. It is a sacred place for them too. Perhaps you have felt it yourself in another situation? Faced with a place so beautiful that you don't even want to breathe in case it disturbs it? Or at the other end of the scale - a place of battle where people have fallen and died and you don't want to commit sacrilege by walking on that ground. Those are my thoughts anyway.'

'That makes perfect sense now you've said it. Are *we* alright in walking through the wood, do you think? I haven't been called.'

'Are you sure about that?' he said and took hold of her hand, shining the torch on the ground in front of them. After a few minutes, he slowed down and nodded to the left. Bridie looked up to see the now familiar glow, much fainter than before. They stopped in front of the tree. Ned got out his hip flask, the one he had filled earlier. He took a sip and then held it up towards the oak tree

'Wassail, Deri. We are thankful for your protection and hope you will bless us all at Midwinter - and bless the seeds that we sow - for the year to come.'

He handed it to Bridie. She took a sip - pure whisky. Made from grain, which was appropriate she supposed but it took her breath away. She tried to remember what he'd said.

'Wassail, Deri. We are thankful for your protection and hope that you will bless us all at

Midwinter and the seeds that are sown, for the coming year.'

She held the flask up towards the tree and it was then that she saw the trunk of the tree change almost imperceptibly into the graceful, insubstantial body of a woman, her arms reaching towards them both like branches. Deri - but older than even this morning. She smiled down benignly at both of them before just as seamlessly, melting into the tree again. Bridie kept watching the pale glow that was all that was left. Eventually, she turned towards Ned to see him staring at her.

'You saw her, didn't you?' he asked

'Yes, did you?'

'No. I felt something but it seems like you're one of the very few over the years that can see her. Consider it a great gift.'

'Oh, I do.' said Bridie, surprised at how honoured she felt, considering a couple of weeks ago, she'd have laughed at all this. Reluctantly she turned away and they walked back home in silence, punctuated only by a few words to the dogs. He did grab hold of her hand again though, which possibly embarrassed both of them, as they both stole glances at each other like teenagers on their first date.

Bridie had time to reflect on how working for Ned at Midwinter Hall had changed her life for the better. Not only that, it had changed her whole outlook on life. She may still be a cynic in most walks of life and not afraid to say so either, but she could never again say that she didn't believe in the mystical, the spiritual and okay, the supernatural she supposed. She had wanted proof - she had her proof and now she had faith. Maybe the wrong way to do it but she had reached the same conclusion in the end.

Bridie heaved a big sigh as they came out of the trackway and in full sight of Midwinter Hall, still lit up in the downstairs rooms, giving a homely warmth to the night. The snow still lay on the ground, just thinner than before with tufts of grass poking through here and there.

She would miss this place when she finished in the library. She wondered how long she could make the job eke out. She would miss all the Midwinter family. Mrs H, Henry and Rose, Marcus and Zinnia. She would miss the adorable dogs and their funny little ways – and Bessie. Most of all, she would miss Ned.

She turned to look at him at the same moment as he turned to look at her. Flustered, she just spat the first thing out, that came into her mind.

'So…Zinnia and Marcus?'

She said it mostly as a distraction but speaking it out loud made her realise that there could possibly be something in it.

Ned smiled and nodded.

'Nothing for definite because they both seem to be keeping it to themselves but- probably.'

'I've only just noticed, you know I'm not very observant?'

'I would say you're very sharp - but perhaps not where romance is concerned?' he finished, looking down at his boots.

They had reached the porch with its fairy lights round the edges. Ned let the dogs inside into the warmth, leaving the door open. They turned to look at the trees.

'You've performed miracles this Christmas Bridie. I didn't think I'd ever celebrate Christmas again, but you've shown me that life must go on.'

'I'm just so glad you've all had a good time. I think your dad would have been pleased.'

'I agree' he said, squeezing her hand and then he bent down to turn the tree lights off.

'No! Not yet.'

He turned to look at her, surprised - and she didn't know what to say, apart from that she didn't want this night to end. She looked at the trees still sparkling in front of the Hall.

'I think we ought to have one more carol before we switch the lights off.'

'Oh no, not me' he put his hands up as if to fend the dreaded event off. He saw Bridie's crestfallen face and quickly said. 'but why don't you sing one? You have a beautiful voice.'

'You're too kind,' she gave a mock bow 'but it's not the same by yourself.'

'What's your favourite carol?' he said after a moment.

She screwed her face up, thinking.

'The Coventry Carol, you know, the Lullay Lullay one. I absolutely love the tune but the words and the concept are both awful so that's out. I don't want to go to sleep thinking of that. So, probably Silent Night.'

'You can sing that by yourself, can't you? I'm staying here with you so you don't seem completely mad.'

She laughed.

'And just for that, I will punish you' she said.

She didn't want him to see her face as she sang, an unaccustomed outbreak of shyness for Bridie, so she turned away from him. She looked out at the darkness beyond the festive trees and thought about today, tonight - and this remarkable place.

'Silent night, Holy night, All is calm, All is bright.'

Her pure voice soared over the tops of the trees and reached every corner of Midwinter including the woods and the fields around it. When she'd finished the first verse, she couldn't sing any more as she felt choked up.

Without a word, Ned put his arms around her, pulling her gently towards him and enveloping her, her cheek resting on his shoulder. While she couldn't see his face, he spoke.

'You shouldn't go home tomorrow. It's still too bad out there' he paused, 'in fact, I don't want you to go home at all. Stay here... tomorrow at least. We could have dinner, just the two of us.' he finished in a hoarse whisper.

She pulled away from him, looking up at him.

'I don't want to go either. Dinner sounds lovely.' She smiled happily. Oh, so happily.

'And Bridie- I know you don't believe in it - for you at least - but I do.'

His lips came slowly down to meet hers, their eyes holding onto each other's until they closed. His hand grasped her hair at the back of her head and she gave herself into him more. His kisses were more urgent and she grabbed his coat collar so they were pressed against each other. Then a strange, sighing noise made them both break apart.

They looked at each other and then down at the threshold where two dogs sat very quietly with faintly puzzled expressions and their heads on one side.

'Oh god' exclaimed Ned putting his hand over his eyes in frustration. 'Come on then, bedtime.'

He stopped in alarm.

'I meant - the dogs. You know - when I said....'

A snort emerged from Bridie who then doubled over with laughter.

'Bridie Emms, you're impossible!'

He laughed and kissed her once more on the lips before he took the dynamic duo back into the kitchen.

*

As Bridie got into her bed, she remembered what he had said inside the porch. 'I know you don't believe in it, for you at least?'

True love! She *had* said that hadn't she? In her long list of things she didn't believe in, she had said that she didn't believe in true love, at least for her. Was that what he meant? If so, she had meant in her life before Midwinter. That was no longer the case, was it? That was then and this was now.

Chapter 31

Boxing day.

It was seldom that the dogs barked. They would probably have let you in the Hall if you were dressed in a striped t-shirt, a beret, a black 'Lone Ranger' mask, and carrying a sack over your shoulder.

Now, however, the cacophony woke Bridie up. She could distinguish a loud knocking underneath the barking contest and realised that it was morning even though it was only just starting to get light. She dashed to the stairs, pulling a jumper over her nightie and then she saw that Ned was already answering the door. He stood on the doorstep barefoot, in just a pair of jeans, his hair stuck up on end.

She reached the hallway at the same time as Mrs H, who had on a peacock-blue quilted dressing gown and wore rollers in her hair. A man stood on the front doorstep, quite unrepentant at waking the household at such an early hour on Boxing Day morning.

'Haven't got you up, have I?'

As if the state of undress wouldn't have answered that question, thought Bridie.

'Thought I'd better take the chance while the roads are a bit better.' the man continued 'More snow forecast in the next couple of days.'

'The chance to...?' puzzled Ned.

'The donkeys, I've brought them' he said simply.

They all popped their heads out of the door to where he pointed at the Donkey Sanctuary's two-donkey transporter, standing near to the top greenhouse.

'Oh yes, that's great but - it seems like you might have to take them to another field instead now, if that's all right?'

'Well now, I've already put them in the paddock behind the house. The man at the stables was just turning your horse out, so I put them in with her.'

Ned's face was a picture.

'With Bessie?'

'If that's what you call her, yes.'

'Was she... alright?'

'Seemed it. She right took to them in fact, licking their ears and fussing over them, like they'd been out on the razz all night and had just got home safe.'

'She was all right? Not stressed?' Ned repeated.

'Looked happy enough to me' the man said, starting to look a little worried.

Ned put his feet in his boots and started to go outside. Mrs H called him back, holding his coat out after him.

'Ned! You'll catch your death!'

Spoilsport, thought Bridie. She was quite enjoying the sight of the toned body.

'I'll take it for him' she said, putting on her own boots and coat and following him. The donkey man followed her at his own slow pace. As she reached the paddock and handed the coat to him, she followed Ned's line of vision.

Dawn was breaking and in the middle of the paddock, she saw one donkey happily kicking her back legs in glee while the other stood with her muzzle against Bessie's when the old horse bent down to meet it. The donkeys changed places with the other coming for a 'getting to know you' nuzzle, while the other explored the nearer boundaries of the paddock.

Then to the amazement of Ned and of Marcus, who had turned Bessie out first thing, all three of them galloped around the field, according to their own abilities, as none of them were youngsters. They looked exceedingly happy, gambolling in the snow, breath coming out of their nostrils into the half-dark air.

'It seems' Ned couldn't tear his eyes from them, 'that there will be no cleaning of Zinnia's brick shed today. They can share our stables as arranged but all at one end now - so that Bessie isn't separated from her adopted children.'

Suddenly he smiled, his face lighting up and the other two smiled as well. Marcus put his hand on Ned's shoulder and Bridie just beamed at him, enjoying the supremely delighted look on his face.

The donkey man just looked on without a clue what was going on and wondered if their strange behaviour was due to hangovers.

*

'You should have seen them' Ned reported down the telephone. 'In fact, come down now Zinnia, I'll send Marcus up for you.'

He had turned at this and winked at Bridie.

The donkey man - who actually had a name and was called Simm - had been directed to the back kitchen door and had emerged half an hour later, full of tasty bacon sandwich and hot coffee to set him up for the drive home, courtesy of Mrs H.

*

Zinnia, who had spent ten minutes watching and petting the donkeys and Bessie, now sat in the kitchen having exactly the same, along with the rest of the household. Mrs H, now in her more familiar white overall in which she was happiest, was being kept busy. The cold weather, the excitement and yes, let's face it, the hangovers, had made them extremely hungry and they all had seconds. Zinnia took another sip of coffee and spoke.

'I can't believe, after all the fuss we made, that the animals have sorted it all out for themselves. Once I had made my mind up, I was quite looking forward to having those two up in…our field.'

'Strangely enough' grinned Ned, 'I already explained the situation to Simm, who says to tell you that there are plenty more donkeys for you to adopt. I've told him that, when the weather is a bit better - and if you're agreeable- I'll run you over there and you can pick out another couple for 'our field''

They laughed without a hint of the awkwardness that was there before Christmas.

'And hopefully, by that time we will have cleaned the shed out' she said

'We'll all be very willing, but I'm sure Marcus will help you anyway.'

Ned looked sideways at Zinnia who swiped him lightly over the head with a placemat and laughed. Even Marcus joined in with a deep-throated chuckle.

It seemed that this, whatever it was, had been an open secret amongst the residents of the Hall for a while. Bridie felt a bit left out until she realised that, until a couple of days ago, she hadn't even been a resident. She wasn't now, come to think of it.

Her heart seemed to drop into her stomach when she thought that soon, apart from her temporary job, she wouldn't be part of this comforting community anymore.

When Bridie and Zinnia were helping to wash up, Bridie as tactfully as ever, asked the older woman outright if she and Marcus were a couple. Zinnia coloured up.

'Oh no. Not as such anyway. Depends on what you mean. I suppose. We enjoy each other's company and we found we have a lot in common. We both have pagan beliefs and we both love Nature and folklore. We both have a great love for music, especially folk music. In fact–'

She stopped and Bridie frowned.

'Go on' she said. 'You can't leave me hanging!'

Zinnia laughed.

'I don't know if you have heard but Emrys and I formed a duo, singing folk songs in small venues in Wales. We gave up the public singing when we came up here and of course, then he became ill. I have to say that I missed it very much.

'When I found out that Marcus played the violin and played it so well too' she said proudly, 'it was like fate. So much so that after a couple of years of performing to the four walls of my dining kitchen, we feel ready to venture forth. We are booked into the local on the Duffield Road, -The Falcon - for the New Year's Eve entertainment.'

'Wow, that's brilliant. Well done Zinnia, for carving a new life for yourself.'

'Will you come to see us? Marcus is still a bit nervous about performing in public, so the more people he knows there the better.'

'Of course I will, I'd be pleased to'

Just then there was another knock at the door.

'Busy Boxing Day this is. It's usually so quiet.' complained Mrs H - but Bridie knew that feeding people was her mission in life and it made her happy. If whoever was knocking could be dragged in for something to eat, it would make her day.

In the event, it was the Wall brothers, who owned the oil suppliers. Nobody else would have turned out on a Boxing Day, but these men were friends of Ned's family. They socialised with the people who worked at the Midwinter nurseries. They were part of the local community and they didn't like letting people down.

'Adam, Ian - come in!' Ned shook their hands and pulled them into the kitchen.

'I'm sorry we couldn't get through' they apologised.

'Nobody can blame you for that' said Zinnia.

'Maybe you could deliver to Henry and Rose first?' Ned suggested.

'But before you do, have a piece of homemade pork pie and a turkey sandwich - and a nice cup of tea.' said Mrs H, her happiness complete.

Bridie caught a movement - Marcus coming back from the hallway where he'd left his violin last night when he saw Zinnia home. An idea came into her head. As with all those sort of ideas, they manifested themselves in a series of words. Duo. Performing in a pub. Marcus. Still a bit nervous. In public. The words created a whirlwind in her head and it all came out in a rush from her mouth without any forethought at all. She generally trusted to luck.

Chapter 32

An Impromptu Performance

'I think we may have musical entertainment while you eat' she said, nodding at Marcus who stopped dead halfway across the kitchen to the back door. Was this too much? The wheels were in motion now so - too late.

'Zinnia and Marcus are playing at The Falcon on New Year's Eve and it would be a great idea for them to give us a preview of one of their songs.'

This would throw Marcus in at the deep end so that he would feel better on the actual night. Or not, she thought, looking round at the vaguely horrified faces of everyone except for Adam and Ian, who merely looked intrigued.

Zinnia recovered first and giving Bridie a look which she hoped meant she understood, said,

'The Oak and the Ash, Marcus?' and went to stand in front of the fire. After a moment's pause, Marcus went to join her. Lifting the violin under his chin he took a deep, shaky breath and counted the beat in with his foot. One, two, three, FOUR.

'Oh the Oak and the Ash and the bonnie ivy tree,

How I wish once again in the North I could be.'

Marcus's foot kept time hesitantly at first, but soon his boot was thumping on the kitchen floor as his arm moved up and down at the elbow pushing the tune out of his fiddle.

Zinnia's voice was confident and melodic and they made a perfect duo, glancing at each other periodically and smiling as if sharing a rather nice secret.

Soon everyone was joining in the beat, clapping hands and stamping their feet too. When the song slowed down on the last line, everyone whistled and cheered.

'You're so good!' said Bridie with feeling, giving a delighted Zinnia a hug and looking over at an unusually animated Marcus.

Zinnia leaned forward.

'Thank you.' she whispered in Bridie's ear, 'I think he'll be all right now, don't you?'

Bridie smiled with relief.

Soon after this, everyone went about their own business. The brothers went off to deliver their oil in case the snow did arrive later and Zinnia went off to open the gate for them after they had delivered to Rose Cottage.

*

Bridie and Ned kept occupied the rest of the day. They moved all the hay from the stalls where they'd had originally planned to put the donkeys and brought it down to the freshly cleaned double stall next to Bessie's. Ned had planned to put them in the two small stalls at the other end, as far away from Bessie as he could, but this new development had changed things. The two donkeys were used to sharing a stall so this would make the transition easier. There was a wall between Bessie's ample stall and the donkeys but she could hear them - and see them too when they all put their heads over the low walls at the end to look out over the passageway to the stable yard beyond.

Ned kept running out to check the inhabitants of the paddock, worried that at any time, Bessie would reject the new arrivals or become stressed. Yet each visit just confirmed the blissful equine friendship.

It seemed funny that these two donkeys, no longer in the flush of youth, were acting like skittish children around Bessie. Bessie too, this old horse who had never had foals of her own, had started to mother them right from the off.

'It's amazing, isn't it?' breathed Ned as he watched them, already inseparable, in the field.

Bridie didn't say anything for a moment., deep in thought until she felt Ned's enquiring eyes on her.

'It is.' she smiled 'it's almost like a Christmas miracle.'

'There's a lot of that going about this year' he grinned, turning towards her.

Marcus came over to help them and they all ended up leading the donkeys, through to their new home, bedding them down next to Bessie and giving them a feed.

Henry and Rose surprised them by turning up to meet the new arrivals.

'They're a couple of sweethearts, aren't they?' came Henry's gruff voice from behind them. 'one grey, one brown.'

'What are their names?' added Rose 'Have they already got them?'

'They have' replied Ned, 'and we wouldn't change them even if we could as they fit in perfectly with the rest of the Bs'

'Lumped in with the hairy animals now am I?' said Bridie as Rose looked puzzled.

Ned continued.

'Bessie, Bonnie, Beauty - and the worst behaved one, Bridie.' A deep laugh rumbled through his chest.

'You can mock if you like, but... Actually, you can't mock if you like' she said huffily, spoiling it with a giggle.

Henry and Rose exchanged amused glances.

Marcus left and the rest of them watched as the newcomers and the old hand settled down for the evening. Bessie kept going to the end of her stable to check on them. One whinny brought Bonnie and Beauty trotting to the end of the stall to see their new mum before getting back to the important task of eating.

'I'll see you back down to your cottage' offered Ned. 'It will be warm and toasty now you've got the range working for the heating.'

'It's wonderful' said Rose, 'but we haven't suffered too much, especially with spending our Christmas day up at yours. We're not going back just yet anyway. We're collecting Mrs H.'

'Oh!' Ned looked surprised and Henry looked a bit embarrassed.

'I'm mebbe not supposed to say, if she hasn't asked you yet. She said it'd be all right?'

'Yes of course it's alright. In fact, I insisted she had today off. She took it as a personal insult.'

They all looked at each other wryly, acknowledging this fact.

'We were going to invite Marcus too, but I expect he's at....'

'Yes, I've just told him to make himself scarce too, although he's been helping us today with the donkeys. He's going to eat at Zinnia's now she's got the heating back. It's so hard to get you all to stop working!' he said in exasperation.

'We enjoy working, especially for someone who puts far more hours in than we do' noted Henry, thinking that he'd maybe look in on the greenhouses on the way back if Rose didn't stop him with one of her 'looks'.

'I've stopped working' said Bridie quite happily 'I haven't been in the library, apart from using the laptop a couple of times, since the 22nd'

'Maybe you haven't been cataloguing books, but you've been baking, preparing and serving in and from the kitchen for Mrs H. You've been shovelling snow to the cottage to clear a path for these two reprobates. You've been collecting stray neighbours to come for Christmas dinner, decorating the house and the

White Pines with Christmas lights and greenery, and then finally you've been cleaning out stables. I think you've done your fair share of work, don't you?'

'Hear, hear' said Henry while Bridie blushed and thought how Ned seemed to inspire you to work for him, to put yourself out for him - and he didn't expect anybody to do something that he wouldn't do himself. The people at the Hall and the Nurseries were happy in their work and, as Henry said, Ned worked harder than anyone.

They all walked around to the kitchen door where they were fairly certain they would find Mrs H.

'I'll come down for her later, to see her back up in the dark.'

'It's a clear track now, with all that rock salt you put on. It's not freezing today either, so we can both see her up to the Hall. She could have stayed in our little spare bedroom but she's like us - she likes to sleep in her own bed on a night.'

'I've just got a few more things to do and then I'll be with you' said Mrs H, as they opened the door to a warm blast of air from the kitchen.

'Come through all of you and have a drink with me before you go' said Ned.

'We're all on non-alcoholic beverages after last night' said Mrs H in a superior tone.

'It's all right you saying it like that' spluttered Ned. 'It was mostly from those lethal concoctions that you and Rose make. They could be used as weapons of mass destruction, flattening your enemy by fermented fruit!'

'You didn't have to drink it, young man.'

Ned looked at Bridie, his hands held towards her with an air of entreaty.

'What would they have done if I'd refused to drink it?'

'They'd have had your guts for garters' she said, agreeing completely. The homemade wine was obviously a yearly ritual, even if the normal Christmas celebrations weren't observed until this year.

'Slander!' said Mrs H in mock horror as they all laughed. Bridie enjoyed the banter between them all. It made her feel like she belonged somehow.

'Right, now,' Mrs H checked the warming oven, 'I've left instructions here on the table. It's a put-together meal because I don't like waste but I think it'll be tasty, just the same. The table's set in the dining room again as it's a shame to use it just for one day. Enjoy your meal.'

Mrs H grabbed her coat and hat and all three of them had strange smiles on their faces as they went out of the back door. Bridie knew immediately that they'd been set up. Ned looked perplexed but turned and grinned at her. After all, he had said last night on the doorstep that they should have dinner together, just the two of them. Now it was about to come true.

Chapter 33

Boxing Day evening

Ned had finished putting the food on the table, according to Mrs H's instructions. He was wearing a smart, dark blue shirt and off-white chinos. He felt ridiculously unsure of himself, like he was sixteen again and on his first date. Although, thinking of his first date- a greasy-skinned and extremely buxom, gung-ho sort of girl that his father had set him up with - Bridie was in no way comparable.

Looking back on the short time she had been at Midwinter, he couldn't believe the impact she had made on him. He hadn't realised how much of a decline he had fallen into. His work was God and real life didn't matter.

Bridie had taught him that real life mattered so much. Although he needed to work for a living of course and that should be taken seriously, she had shown him how to enjoy life and see the humour in it. She had taught him how to laugh again.

He wasn't sure how ready he was to face real life - and real relationships - but all he knew was that Bridie had to be part of this new life. It was a maelstrom of feelings that whirled around his head as he opened the dining room door and stepped out into the hallway.

There was a noise at the top of the stairs and he looked up towards the landing. Bridie moved slowly down towards him, her hand skimming the banister as she glided downstairs. She was wearing a green dress, an unusual shade, with beads that shone like diamonds. If Ned had any doubts before now, they had been dispelled in that instant as he gazed at this stubborn, outspoken, unique, wonderful and sublimely beautiful woman who stepped down towards him now.

*

Bridie felt butterflies in her stomach. Hell - she felt like Alien was going to burst out any minute - although in a soppy, benevolent way, if that was possible.

She had put on the dress she hadn't dared put on for Christmas Day. It suited her perfectly. The leaf-green bodice clung to her body showing her perfect curves. The green chiffon overskirt, reaching just above her ankles, glistened with sparkling beads. She had to admit to herself that it went perfectly with her tumbling red curls.

It wasn't 'her'. She didn't do glamour. Yet as she took in Ned's expression, she realised that perhaps it could be her. Possibly she had a glamorous side to her after all. Or maybe she just wanted to look her best for the right person.

As she reached the last step, her eyes locked on Ned's and when she saw the glazed look in them, there were a few moments of weightlessness until she came down to earth and held out her arm. He kissed her hand and led her into the dining room, which was just as magical as the previous day and the contents just as delicious.

There was a ham and leek quiche and a turkey and ham raised pie. There were new potatoes with parsley, garden salad and salads of red cabbage, coleslaw and beetroot.

For later there was a cheese board with Wensleydale and cranberry - and Yorkshire Dale End cheddar from the North Yorkshire Moors, accompanied by Mrs H's special date and apple chutney. A big bowl of apples was displayed and the cold desserts were already there alongside it - Irish cream profiteroles and a tiramisu.

The table had been laid just in the middle section. A snow-white tablecloth had two small candelabra at each side that threw flickering shadows across the table as they sat down opposite each other. The fire, built up by Ned earlier, crackled merrily, throwing just enough heat out.

They sat in silence as they reached towards the dishes to fill their plates. It was obvious they both felt a little awkward. There was no wonder as things had escalated so quickly. In the space of a week, they had gone from being boss and temporary employee to something altogether different.

In the middle of transferring the potatoes to their plates, Ned caught Bridie's eye. She grinned at him and they both burst out laughing. The awkwardness was over. After a few seconds. There was a whining noise at the door.

'They were fast asleep in the kitchen when I left them' Ned apologised. 'Do you mind if I let them in?'

'Of course I don't mind. They won't want to be left out.'

Ned got up and the two dogs flew in. Tam, sniffed at Bridie to say hello but Tink stopped dead, staring at her. Bridie could swear that the little dog didn't recognise her, all glammed up. After a cautious approach and a sniff, she seemed happy that this person was indeed the same one who normally dressed in jumpers and jeans, so she went to join Tam in front of the fire with an untroubled mind.

'You do realise that Mrs H - and probably the rest of them - have planned this, don't you?' Ned asked her.

'Oh yes. I realised it as Mrs H scuttled off to Rose Cottage in a hurry. You don't mind, do you? There's nothing much else to do is there?'

'Charming!' he replied. 'I'm glad I'm here as a distraction to stop you from getting bored.'

Oops, she thought, until she heard his low laugh. She most definitely wasn't bored. They fell into easy conversation, going into their past lives in more detail than before. He asked if there had been anyone special in her life to which she could honestly answer,

'No, no one special at all. What about you?'

'No one special, even remotely, for me.'

The cogs in Bridie's mind turned over for a minute as she remembered the week after she'd started here.

'There was a woman a few weeks ago, long dark hair, face make-up by 'St. Tropez Orange', lips like they'd been blown up by a bicycle pump...'

There was a splutter as Ned nearly choked on a profiterole.

'I see you know who I mean from the description.'

'I do' he grinned at her.

'I got the impression that *she* was your girlfriend.'

'Yes, so did she. I had to put her right. She was relentless once she'd set her sights on me.'

'I'm glad you said that.'

'Why?' he said, smiling with a hint of mischief, 'did you meet her?'

'Briefly. I may have said a few friendly words to her in passing.'

'Friendly?' asked Ned, still smiling.

'Well, a few friendly words of advice really' said Bridie.

At this Ned started laughing.

'What' Bridie said. Surely the woman hadn't told him of their 'encounter' in the library. The Bride of Frankenstein had followed her in after she'd collected a coffee from Mrs H and was taking it back to her desk. She *couldn't* have said anything. For a start, it would have put the woman herself in a bad light. Come to think of it though, she hadn't seen her since that day. Ned was laughing again, damn him.

'What!' she repeated, throwing her arms up in frustration.

'I was there. In the library.'

'No you weren't' Bridie answered. looking confused.

'I had gone in when you were in the kitchen. I was looking for something at the far side of the end bookcase. You wouldn't have seen me and it was too late to announce my presence when it all kicked off.'

'You heard everything then?' said Bridie, thinking that, if so, it was a wonder she hadn't been asked to leave then and there.

'It's all imprinted on my brain.' He lifted one side of his mouth, trying not to smile. 'I heard her telling you to 'stop flirting with me as you were making it obvious - and what would Sir Edward want with someone like you – and anyway, he belongs to *me*!'

Bridie's eyes widened but she kept quiet. Ned went on.

'And I heard you say 'Jesus, don't get your knickers in a twist dear. I'm not flirting and I'm not after him. Yes, he *is* gorgeous, but he's my boss. You need to tame that green-eyed monster because if you don't - My God, I feel so sorry for him and the life of hell that he'll have with you.'

A low chuckle sounded in his throat.

'I particularly liked the 'gorgeous' bit.'

'You're enjoying this, aren't you?' she asked, smiling herself now that she knew he wasn't angry. 'She'd obviously come here to vet me and was disappointed that I wasn't 70 and fat. I'm sorry if I made her leave- I haven't seen her since.'

'No, you're not! Anyway, it wasn't you who made her leave, it was me. You stormed out and she went after you. I caught her before she reached the kitchen door and she realised I'd just come out of the library, so the game was up. I took her into the sitting room and said 'How dare she speak to you like that- and if you *had* been flirting, you had a perfect right as I didn't *belong* to her. I didn't *belong* to anyone.' Then I asked her to leave and not come back.'

'Wow!' she said with feeling. 'You do like to keep your secrets, don't you? Thank you for sticking up for me.'

'The thing is you see...' he stopped talking- the awkwardness had returned. He began again. '...that if you had shown any interest in me, I would have been very happy. And when I said that I didn't *belong* to anyone - I would have quite liked it if I'd belonged to you. If we belonged together. What I'm trying to say is- '

'I know what you're trying to say' Bridie jumped in, 'I think, to be honest, we've both been fighting this feeling ever since I came to Midwinter Hall, haven't we? At least I have.'

'Oh Bridie, thank goodness for you telling it like it is' he laughed. 'Come on, let's go and have an Irish coffee in front of the Yule fire and discuss this further.'

Chapter 34

New beginnings.

'You thought the same thing about Bessie as I did didn't you?'

Ned was sitting next to Bridie on the settee. They had their arms around each other with no awkwardness at all. It seemed the most natural thing in the world.

'I did think it was a coincidence that she and Deri met the day before she accepted the donkey's company but it probably was just that. Let's not read too much into it.'

'Oho! And here's me thinking we'd converted you into a fully-fledged believer after your experiences. A new recruit to these pagan backwaters of Yorkshire.'

'I have to say that I have had proof handed to me on a plate, so unless this last week has been some strange dream and I'm going to wake up from it soon, then I have to believe.'

'Do you want to wake up from the dream?'

'No, I want it to go on forever. Perhaps not cut off with the snow but even that has added to the magic. If I had to be isolated from the outside world, I can't think of a better place to be and no better people to be stranded with.'

He leaned across and kissed her gently.

'It's been the best week of my life' he whispered, 'I don't want you to go.'

Her heart dropped as she remembered.

'I'll have to go when the library work is done. As much as I would try to spin it out, eventually…'

'Not just the work, I don't want you to go from here, ever.'

'You're not planning to imprison me in the attic again, are you?' Bridie could curse her mistimed humour sometimes.

'If that's what it takes' he laughed, twirling an imaginary 'panto villain' moustache and wiggling his eyebrows.

'You won't have to, I'll stay willingly' she smiled and kissed him back, snuggling into his shoulder before adding,

'You'll have to find me another job to do, I won't be a kept woman.'

'There will be plenty to do, you've already shown you're not afraid of hard work. I could do with some help in the flower fields next year.'

'That sounds lovely - and I could help Mrs H?'

'If she lets you...'

'If she lets me' Bridie agreed. They knew the kitchen was Mrs H's domain.

'She thinks a lot about you.'

'The feeling is entirely mutual.'

'You've fitted right in here' he said, standing and pulling her up. He turned her to face him.

'What are you doing for New Year?'

'I've been invited to so many parties, I'm spoilt for choice' she said with a lift of her eyebrow before she realised she had thought about spending New Year with her friend, Chantal. She would understand - she had been trying to introduce her to various unsuitable men for years, so she'd be over the moon about Ned. She would go and see her soon to make up for it.

'I was wondering' he said 'if you'd like to go up to Scotland with me? For Hogmanay?'

'Will I have to play the bagpipes?' Shut up Bridie, she thought, take things seriously for once.

'No, but you might have to listen to them. Just down the hill from Elise's castle, there's a small village with one pub - and the piper plays outside there at midnight before everyone piles back into the pub to get warm and even more inebriated. We can't miss it.'

Two things jumped out at Bridie to worry her. Firstly 'Elise' and then 'Castle'.

'Elise, your sister you mean? I haven't even met her yet, are you sure they won't mind me staying there?'

'They won't be there. She, with her husband Alistair and the children, will be away sunning themselves on a Caribbean island. There will be just the two of us. You'll have to meet them at some point though. They're coming here when they come back from the holiday.'

'She'll want her bedroom back then won't she?'

'I hope it will be free before then' he grabbed her hands and squeezed them.

She hoped so too and at least some of the worry dissolved.

'And when you say 'Castle'?' she said quietly.

'I mean, Castle' he laughed. 'Elise is married to the Earl of Monmuir.'

Something completely random came galloping into Bridie's mind.

Oh God, I've been wearing the Countess of Monmuir's knickers!

*

They stood on the top step of Midwinter Hall. The snow was falling gently again but it didn't seem to matter anymore.

Tam and Tink had to be called in twice. They were both having a snowflake-catching contest, jumping up to try to catch them in their mouths. Eventually, they flew up the steps leaving Bridie and Ned, arm in arm to have a last look at the lights on the trees- and a reverent glance over to the Silent Wood- before they too came back into the golden warmth of the sitting room. The Yule log still burned, guaranteeing good luck for the year to come. Ned pulled Bridie over to the candlelit window. He stood back, watching her. She was so beautiful, the green dress showing off her long red curls. He softly stroked them.

Bridie looked at the gorgeous man opposite her, tall, blue-eyed with his blonde hair curling over the dark blue shirt. Best of all, he was looking at her with love in his eyes.

Almost as one, they reached for each other and kissed – even more passionately than before. When they broke off, her hands grasped his shoulders and his arms encircled her waist. They slowly began moving as one, dancing to the spellbinding music that was only inside their heads.

The dogs, from their place near the fire, looked over at them, wondering why these crazy humans were slowly turning round in circles. Then they looked across at each other contentedly before putting their heads on their paws and dreaming sweet dreams.

Epilogue

The snow that was forecast for the next day had arrived. Not thick enough to stop the gritters and snow ploughs from doing their jobs - but enough to give Bridie and Ned an excuse to spend time together at Midwinter Hall for a while longer - not that they needed one now.

It was New Year's Eve and the mellow morning light shone on the Hall, giving it a welcoming appearance. Ned was making sure everything in the greenhouses was as it should be. The Midwinter Nurseries workers would be back in five days and it just needed to tick over until then.

He knew, however much he told Henry to just check just once or twice - and then only if the weather was good, that Henry would spend most of his time in his little glass 'den' at the end of the top greenhouse, brewing a cuppa from his kettle and telling his rows of seedlings to 'buck up a bit, you should be looking livelier than that'

Rose would probably walk up to the Hall at the same time to have coffee and a scone with Mrs H. Ned had told Mrs H to try and relax and read or maybe watch TV, only to be met with an 'And where do you suppose all the baking will magically come from when your sister and the family arrive?'

Ned had given up. They were all strong characters with minds of their own and had survived, more than survived - thrived, for all these years without listening to a word he said. And now, here he was, head over heels in love with another of the same ilk. He smiled, as he often did when he thought of Bridie.

He had been so happy when she agreed to spend New Year with him in Scotland. It had all happened so quickly - a whirlwind romance - but like he told her, when you know it's right, why hold back? He hoped that she would agree to make it more permanent while they were up at the castle and he patted the inside pocket of his jacket for the tenth time to make sure the tiny leather box was still there.

Zinnia and Marcus had readily agreed to look after Bonnie, Beauty and Bessie till they got back. Zinnia said that she had to get into practice anyway for when her own donkeys came in two weeks' time.

All he had to do now was to take this bottle of champagne to Marcus and wish him good luck on his folk singing debut at The Falcon. He had apologised because he and Bridie couldn't be there to cheer them on but hoped that he could share this bottle with Zinnia afterwards to celebrate their success.

Then, as the Land Cruiser was already packed, he had only to pile the dogs and Bridie into it and head towards Scotland.

*

Bridie had taken Tam and Tink for a last walk before the journey. She knew where she would go, even if her legs hadn't automatically led her there. She wanted one last word. The dogs ran ahead. They knew where they were going too.

Bridie turned around, just before she lost sight of Midwinter Hall and watched the snow steadily sliding off the roof in the sunshine. She had come to love this place, not just the Hall but the whole of Midwinter. In such a short time, she had grown so very fond of the animals and of the people who lived and worked around here. None more so than Ned.

What had she said so flippantly on Christmas Night? She didn't believe in true love? That statement might have been valid once – but no longer.

She had known that, while making fun of Ned's sometimes serious ways and while complaining about his miserable attitude to Christmas, she had been falling in love with him all along. That he had felt exactly the same about her had been like a dream come true.

She looked up and saw that Tam and Tink had already taken up their stations at the entrance to the Silent Wood. Tam gazed knowingly down the woodland path, as though she knew secrets that no one else did. Tink stared up at her companion and tried to adopt the same intelligent expression but failed miserably. Bridie grinned and hugged them both before she went down the path.

There was no obvious glow. Was she too late? Could she even find the tree now? Gradually, she began to be overtaken by the calm atmosphere that the wood gave out and she just let her feet take her along.

On the right-hand side of the wood, where she had first seen the glowing tree, she stopped and examined a tall, stout oak. There was no light coming from inside it and no tree nymph in a fluorescent green dress but she felt instinctively that this was Deri's tree. She leaned towards the trunk putting her arms at either side of it. She put her head against the bark and closed her eyes.

'Deri' she whispered softly, 'I've come to say goodbye. No, not goodbye because I hope to see you again - but I think what I really want to say is - thank you.

'Thank you firstly for opening me up to a whole new world which I had refused to believe in before I came here. That of the supernatural, the spiritual, the mystical, the magical. I now believe in the existence of things that we have no idea about and possibly never will. I have faith.

Mainly, I want to thank you for helping me to belong to Midwinter. It's strange, I feel as though I have always belonged here, but now, I feel it more than ever. I don't know how but I believe you've had a hand in that. You are helping us all here, humans and animals, to make the right decisions, both for us – and for the well-being and continuation of Midwinter.

'And I promise that, if I am lucky enough to stay here with Ned, for a while at least and maybe – hopefully - forever, then I will do my best to protect you as you protect Midwinter. I hope...', she wiped away a stray tear, 'I really hope, that I will see you again next year.'

She tightened her arms around the ancient oak and hugged it. She felt some heat against her forehead and she quickly opened her eyes lifting her head back.

There was Deri's face, a faint outline in the tree, yet still having the kind eyes and wise smile of a beautiful old woman. The smile widened now.

'You will' Deri's voice echoed around Bridie's mind, making her laugh out loud with delight. 'You will.'

*

Ned turned at the excited yapping of a Yorkshire terrier trying to keep up with a rocket-like Border Collie and with a red-haired sprinter showing a surprising turn of speed. The sprinter took pity on Tink and picked her up and they all landed in a heap at the same time, at the door of the Land Cruiser.

Ned shook his head with his eyebrows raised. Bridie was flushed with exertion and laughter and the dogs were jumping about with glee.

Mrs H, who had witnessed the manic arrival, was standing at the door, laughing as she waved them off. She shut the door behind her, feeling thankful that things had worked out so well. The old place would be a lot livelier now Bridie was here to stay.

Ned climbed into the driver's seat.

'What on earth have you done to them?' he laughed after the dogs calmed down and settled down in the back, 'I was hoping they'd go to sleep but–'

'They'll be so tired out with the exercise, I'm sure they will be asleep in five minutes. You can thank me later' she grinned.

'Does that mean you'll go to sleep too?'

'No chance' she said 'You're stuck with me for the whole journey.'

'I'm happy to be stuck with you for the rest of my life' he said, kissing her before they made their way out of Midwinter. Meanwhile, the dweller in the Silent Wood slept lightly, until she was needed again.

Acknowledgements

Firstly, I would like to thank my husband Tony and my daughter Lisa, who was then seven years old, for buying me the Reader's Digest 'Folklore, Myths and Legends of Britain' for Christmas long ago. It confirmed my love of folklore and has been used for reference continually ever since to the point where the cover is held together by sellotape!

I would also like to thank my friends Dorothy and Joe Whelan who introduced me to The Donkey Sanctuary in Sidmouth which they have always supported. If you want to show your support too, their website address is www.thedonkeysanctuary.org.uk

There is also a Border Collie rescue operating from Richmond, Yorkshire and their website is www.bordercollierescue.org

I would also like to mention that my parents, to whom this book is dedicated, are nothing like Bridie's parents in this book! They were kind, nurturing parents who brought me up in a house filled with love, for which I am forever grateful.

Thank you once again to my brilliant family who have encouraged me right from the start and continue to do so.

Lastly, I want to thank my readers, who are incredibly supportive with their lovely posts on my Facebook page and their wonderful reviews on Amazon. Thanks to you all for buying the books and taking the time to tell me you like them. It keeps me writing.